# MILLIKEN'S COMPLETE BOOK OF Reading and Writing REPRODUCIBLES

Over **110** Activities for Today's Differentiated Classroom

-4

Compiled by: Sara Inskeep
Cover design: Logo Design Team
Page Layout: Janine M. Chambers

© 2009 Milliken Publishing Company, a Lorenz company, and its licensors.
All rights reserved.

Permission to photocopy the student activities in this book is hereby granted to one teacher as part of the purchase price. This permission may only be used to provide copies for this teacher's specific classroom setting. This permission may not be transferred, sold, or given to any additional or subsequent user of this product. Thank you for respecting copyright laws.

Printed in the United States of America

ISBN 978-1-4291-0465-4

P.O. Box 802 • Dayton, OH 45401
www.LorenzEducationalPress.com

# How to Use This Book . . .

The activities in this book provide an excellent source of reading and writing practice for elementary students. The pages can be used as drill reinforcement or as independent instructional material and are designed to help motivate students to learn through a variety of exercises. The activities in this book are grouped by skill; these skills may overlap more than one grade level and should be used in ways that best meet each student's needs. The reproducibles are created so that a student can work with a minimum of supervision in a classroom or at home. Answer keys have been provided in the back of the book.

EXTRA! EXTRA! When you see this symbol, be sure to check out the "extra" extension activity provided.

## Table of Contents

**Reading Comprehension.** . . . . . . . . . . . . . . . . . . . . . . . 3

**Homophones/Homographs** . . . . . . . . . . . . . . . . . . . . 66

**Writing** . . . . . . . . . . . . . . . . . . . . . . . . . . . . . . . . . . . . 70

# Key Words

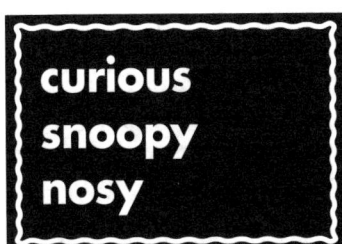

curious
snoopy
nosy

Mother Mouse said to Matt Mouse, "Don't go into the kitchen tonight."

"Why?" asked Matt, but Mother didn't answer.

This made Matt more **curious**. As soon as he could, Matt slipped into the kitchen. He was a **nosy** mouse, and he looked in every nook and cranny. Poking around a corner, **snoopy** Matt saw two huge, yellow, shiny things. Now, the little mouse was scared. He turned and ran back into his home.

A. Read the story. Then fill in the missing words

   1. "Why?" asked Matt. He was _____.
   2. The _____ little mouse saw two yellow things.
   3. The _____ mouse looked in every nook and cranny.

B. Write the key words.

   1. Write the words that rhyme

      **cozy** _____  **furious** _____

      **droopy** _____

   2. When you wonder about something, you are _____.
   3. To be snoopy is to be _____.
   4. Put the key words in alphabetical order. Then write them in the puzzle.

      _____
      _____
      _____

On another sheet of paper, write the next paragraph in the story. What are the huge, shiny, yellow things that Matt sees?

Name _____   Date _____

# Key Words

**dreadful**
**frightening**
**horrible**

"Mother, Mother!" cried Matt Mouse. "I just saw the most **horrible** thing! It was **frightening**!" "Where?" asked Mother.

"In the kitchen," said Matt.

"Didn't I say not to go into the kitchen?" asked Mother.

"Yes, but I am a curious mouse. I was being nosy," replied Matt.

"Tell me what you saw," said Mother as she embraced Matt.

"In a corner, I saw two huge, yellow, shiny things. I was scared," Matt said.

"How **dreadful** for you! You saw the eyes of the new house cat, Zips. Cats can be dangerous for little mice," said Mother.

A. Read the story. Then fill in the missing words.

1. Mother said, "How _____ for you."

2. The two yellow, shiny things were _____.

3. Curious Matt saw a most _____ thing.

B. Write the answers.

1. Put the key words in alphabetical order.

   _____
   _____
   _____

2. Match each key word with its base word.

   horror          frightening
   dread           horrible
   fright          dreadful

Write your own scary story. Use each key word at least one time in your story.

MP5095 - Reading and Writing                Reading Comprehension

Name _____  Date _____

# Key Words

One morning, Mr. White said, "I think there is a mouse in our house. We must get a cat. It must be a **wise** cat and a **clever** one. The cat we need should be sneaky. It takes a **sly** cat to catch a mouse."

Zips heard Mr. White talking. Zips knew he could sneak up on mice. He was looking for a new home. So Zips came to live with Mr. White.

A. Read the story. Then fill in the missing words.

   1. Mr. White wanted a _____ cat.

   2. He said, "It must be a wise cat and a _____ one."

   3. To catch mice, Zips had to be _____.

B. Write the key words.

   1. Write the words that rhyme

   **fly** _____   **size** _____

   **never** _____

   2. Write a key word to finish each common saying.

   _____ as an owl
   _____ as a cat
   _____ as a fox

   3. Put the key words in alphabetical order. Then write them in the puzzle.

   _____
   _____
   _____

   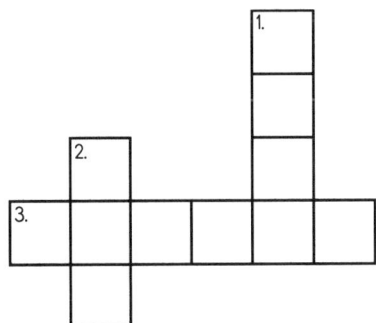

MP5095 - Reading and Writing    5    Reading Comprehension

# Key Words

**gazed
glimpsed
peered**

Zips, the clever cat, set out to catch the mice. He began to sneak around the kitchen looking for the mouse house. At last, he spotted the little hole. "Ah, ha!" he cried. "I have found it."

Zips sat down and looked at the hole. He did not move. He **gazed** into the darkness. Suddenly, he **glimpsed** something move.

"What was that?" he asked himself.

Zips **peered** deeper into the hole. There, staring back at him was the snoopy nose of curious Matt.

A. Read the story. Then fill in the missing words.

1. Zips _____ deeper into the hole.
2. Zips sat and _____ at the hole.
3. Zips _____ something move.

B. Write the base word for each key word.

1. A quick look is a _____.
2. To stare a long time is to _____.
3. To watch or to peer is to _____.

C. Use the base words to fill in the puzzle.

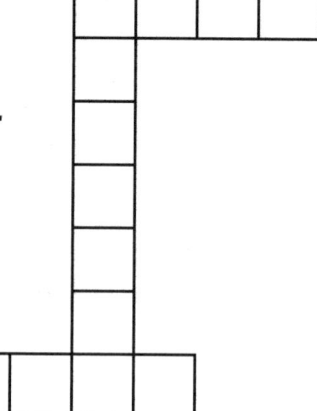

Make a list of other words that describe **seeing**.

# Key Words

fret
worry
complain

Zips began to **worry** Mother Mouse. "I do wish he would go away," she sighed.

"So do I," said Matt. "I can't snoop in the kitchen."

"You stay out of the kitchen. I don't want to have to **fret** about you," Mother warned.

Matt began to **complain**. "But it's no fun in here."

Mother said, "Remember how frightening it was the first time you met that horrible Zips. Be wise. Stay out of the cat's way!"

A. Read the story. Then fill in the missing words.

1. Matt began to _____ that it was no fun.
2. Mother began to _____ about Zips at the door.
3. Mother warned, "I don't want to _____."

B. Write the key words.

1. You might _____ about something if you didn't like it.
2. To worry is to _____.
3. If something bothers you, you often _____ about it.

Write a paragraph about something that worries you. What do you do to help ease your worries?

Name _____ Date _____

# Key Words

**mischief**
**trick**
**prank**

"It may be wise to stay out of Zips' way," thought Matt. "But I want to be clever. I will play a **trick** on that cat. I will get Molly Mouse to help. She likes to play **pranks**, too."

So Matt and Molly met to plan their **mischief**. Matt went to the back door of the mouse house. Molly stayed at the front door where Zips sat. Matt put out his tail. He jiggled it. Zips jumped and turned. Then Molly thumped her tail. Zips ran back and forth between the two little mice. Zips began to worry. He could not catch Matt or Molly. Their game was working.

A. Read the story. Then fill in the missing words.

1. Matt and Molly planned their _____.
2. Matt wanted to play a _____ on Zips.
3. Molly liked to play _____s too.

B. Write the key words.

1. _____ can lead to trouble.
2. A magician does a magic _____.
3. A mean trick is called a _____.

Write a story about a trick or prank you have seen played on someone. How did this person feel about the trick?

# Key Words

**astonishment**
**amaze**
**surprise**

The next day came a big **surprise**. Matt peered out of the mouse house. Zips was not gazing back!

"Where is he?" asked Matt curiously.

"Don't worry. He will be back," said Molly.

"Our clever trick worked," boasted Matt.

"Don't brag too soon. Zips might be hiding."

"Let's go see," said Matt bravely.

The two little mice strolled into the kitchen. To their **astonishment**, Zips just sat and looked at them.

"I give up. Let's be friends and **amaze** everyone," said Zips.

"Cats and mice be friends? That will be a wonder!" laughed Matt.

A. Read the story. Then fill in the missing words.

1. It was a _____ not to see Zips.
2. Cats and mice as friends will _____ everyone.
3. To their _____ , Zips just gazed at them.

B. Fill in the missing words.

1. Write the base word for **astonishment**. _____
2. A magic trick will _____ you.
3. A _____ party can be fun!

Write a paragraph about your most surprising experience. Use at least one of the key words in your paragraph.

# Review

| | | | | |
|---|---|---|---|---|
| curious | mischief | wise | amaze | peered |
| dreadful | fret | glimpsed | nosy | complain |
| clever | frightening | worry | horrible | prank |
| gazed | snoopy | trick | sly | surprise |
| astonishment | | | | |

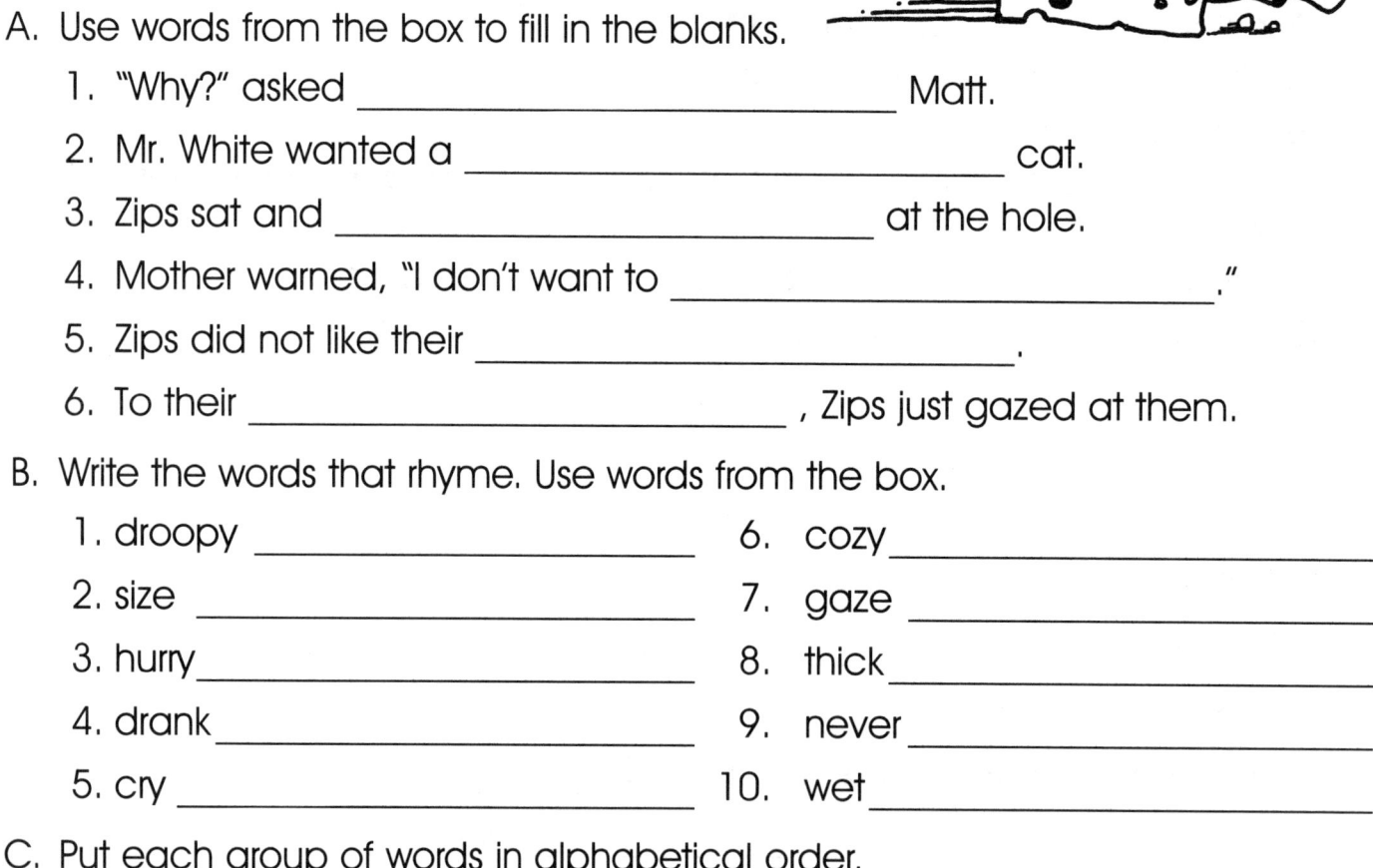

A. Use words from the box to fill in the blanks.

1. "Why?" asked _____ Matt.
2. Mr. White wanted a _____ cat.
3. Zips sat and _____ at the hole.
4. Mother warned, "I don't want to _____."
5. Zips did not like their _____.
6. To their _____ , Zips just gazed at them.

B. Write the words that rhyme. Use words from the box.

1. droopy _____
2. size _____
3. hurry _____
4. drank _____
5. cry _____
6. cozy _____
7. gaze _____
8. thick _____
9. never _____
10. wet _____

C. Put each group of words in alphabetical order.

1. fret, clever, amaze, dreadful

_____

2. peered, nosy, snoopy, mischief

_____

Name _____   Date _____

# Review

3. glimpsed, curious, horrible, frightening

   _____

4. trick, prank, wise, surprise

   _____

D. Use the words from the box on page 10 to complete the puzzle. You will need to add some **-ed** endings.

**Across**
4. to fret
5. to surprise (base word)
8. stared long
9. to grumble
11. horrible
12. peeked in
13. snoopy
14. full of questions
15. smart
16. this can be trouble

**Down**
1. rhymes with set
2. mean trick
3. a magic _____
4. smart
5. full of wonder(d)
6. _____ like a fox
7. nosy
8. looked quickly
10. kind of party

Name_____ Date _____

# Key Words

**launch**
**admiral**
**fleet**

Clint Hill had been an **admiral** in the navy for many years. He was proud of his **fleet** of fine ships. Today, a trim, white motorboat waited at the dock. This was the **launch** that would take him to his command ship. Soon, Admiral Hill would climb aboard his ship and give the command to **launch**. Then, one by one, the huge ships would move slowly out to sea.

A. Read the story. Then fill in the missing words.

1. Admiral Hill was proud of his _____.
2. The _____ would climb aboard his ship.
3. It was time to _____ the fleet.

B. Write in the key words.

1. To set sail is to _____ a ship.
2. Many ships together are called a _____.
3. A motorboat can be a _____.
4. The leader of a fleet is an _____.

C. Fill in the puzzle with the key words.

1. to set sail
2. many ships
3. leader of ships

Write a story about an adventure you would like to have if you were the captain of your own ship. Where would you go? What would you do there?

Name _____  Date _____

# Key Words

**loyal**
**faithful**
**true**

Admiral Hill thought his sailors were very special. They were **loyal** to the admiral and proud to be in his fleet. It was **true**, they were not an ordinary crew. Every sailor was **faithful** in doing the jobs aboard ship. The Admiral's fleet boasted that it was the best on the high seas.

A. Read the story. Then fill in the missing words.

   1. The crew was _____ in doing their jobs.
   2. They were _____ to Admiral Hill.
   3. It was _____ they were not an ordinary crew.

B. Fill in the key words.

   1. Write the words that rhyme.

      **royal** _____   **blue** _____

   2. The opposite of **false** is _____.
   3. Another word for **loyal** is _____.
   4. We should be _____ to our country.

On another sheet of paper, write a story about being **loyal**, **faithful**, and **true** to something or someone.

Name_____ Date _____

# Key Words

**craved
required
desired**

After many days at sea, the men **desired** fresh fruit. The need was so great, they **craved** oranges and bananas. To get the fresh fruit **required** they had to find land. They all watched for signs of land. Admiral Hill paced the deck. Suddenly the look-out called, "Land Ho!" The ships were in sight of an unknown island.

A. Read the story. Then fill in the missing words.

1. The sailors _____ fresh fruit.

2. They _____ oranges.

3. The need to find fruit _____ that they find land.

B. Fill in the key words.

1. Write the word that rhymes with **brave**. _____

2. Write the two key words that rhyme.
   _____

3. To need something is to _____ it.

4. When you crave something, you have a strong _____ for it.

C. After each word, write require for something you really need. Write crave for anything you might want but do not need.

1. candy _____   4. ice cream _____
2. good sleep _____   5. daily bath _____
3. brush teeth _____   6. fresh fruit _____

Write a paragraph on another sheet of paper about your favorite foods. Be sure to use all of the key words.

MP5095 - Reading and Writing     Reading Comprehension

Name_____  Date_____

# Key Words

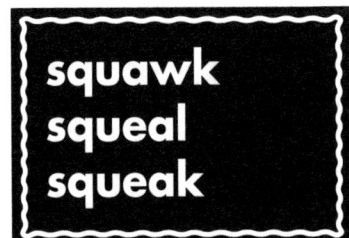

**squawk**
**squeal**
**squeak**

Admiral Hill and a few of the sailors took the launch to the island. The curious sailors ran quickly across the island. One sailor heard a horrible noise. It was the **squeal** of a wild pig. Nearby, a mouse replied with a **squeak**. Just then Admiral Hill heard a loud **squawk**. He looked up and saw a bright-colored parrot. It was sitting in a fruit tree. "This fruit is good," the parrot seemed to say. The sailors happily filled their bags with fresh fruit.

A. Read the story. Then fill in the missing words.

1. The mouse gave a _____ .

2. The pig made a horrible _____ .

3. Admiral Hill heard a loud _____ .

B. Fill in the key words.

1. Write the words that rhyme with

**hawk** _____   **meal** _____

**peek** _____

2. Put the key words in alphabetical order.

_____

C. Use the key words to fill in the puzzle.

1. pig sound
2. parrot sound
3. mouse sound

D. On another paper, write the key word you think each might make.

1. tires stopping suddenly
2. new shoes
3. unhappy children
4. happy children
5. loose floor board

MP5095 - Reading and Writing    15    Reading Comprehension

# Key Words

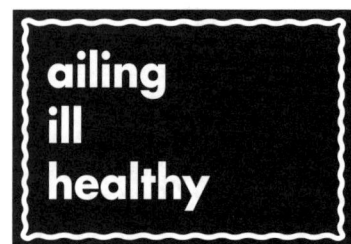

ailing
ill
healthy

The Admiral took many bags of fruit back to the fleet. Some sailors were feeling a little sick. They complained that they were **ailing**. Two of the sailors were very **ill**.

"Don't fret," said the wise Admiral. "Eating fresh fruit will make you feel better. Help yourself."

All the crew ate the fresh fruit from the island. Soon they were **healthy** again.

A. Read the story. Then fill in the missing words.

1. Two sailors were very _____.

2. After eating fruit, the sailors were _____.

3. The wise Admiral fed fruit to his _____ crew.

B. Fill in the key words.

1. If you are a little sick, you are _____.

2. A bad cold makes you feel _____.

3. When you are well, you are _____.

4. Write the base words.

   **ailing** _____    **healthy** _____

C. Use the key words in the puzzle.

   1. a little sick    2. very sick    3. well

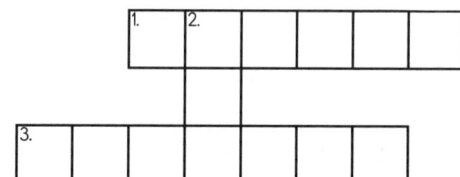

Write a story about the last time you were sick. Be sure to use all of the key words in your story.

MP5095 - Reading and Writing                                    Reading Comprehension

# Review

| launch | required | desire | fleet | ill |
| craved | admiral | squeal | true | shed |
| squeak | faithful | ailing | loyal | scale |
| squawk | healthy | | | |

A. Use the words from the box to fill in the blanks.

1. The mouse gave a _____.
2. Snakes _____ their skins.
3. It was time to _____ the fleet.
4. The sailors _____ oranges.
5. Matt could _____ the wall quickly.
6. The sailors were _____ to Admiral Hill.
7. The _____ crew ate fresh fruit.

B. Write words that rhyme.

1. **royal** _____
2. **blue** _____
3. **saved** _____
4. **desired** _____
5. **hawk** _____
6. **meal** _____
7. **peek** _____
8. **wealthy** _____
9. **male** _____
10. **sailing** _____
11. **pill** _____
12. **red** _____

Use two of the words in the box above to write a sentence about yourself.

Name_____ Date_____

# Key Words

**audio**
**auditorium**
**audience**

Everyone was excited about the special morning program. A real explorer had come to school. All the students were going to the **auditorium** to hear the famous Bill Finder.

The explorer greeted the eager **audience**. "I will share my trip to Hidden Island with you. We will have slides, a film, and a special **audio** tape. The tape has the recorded sounds of unknown animals. I hope you enjoy the program."

A. Read the story. Then fill in the missing words.

1. The students were going to the _____.

2. The explorer would play an _____ tape with the sounds of animals.

3. Boys and girls were the eager _____.

B. Write the correct key word in each blank.

1. People who see and hear a program are the _____.

2. A place to see a program is an _____.

3. You hear sound in the _____ part of a program.

C. Fill in the puzzle using the key words.

1. people
2. sound
3. place

Look up **audio** in the dictionary. Find three more words that use **audio** to make a new word. On another paper, write your new words. Use each one in a sentence.

# Key Words

**starboard**
**deck**
**bow**

The explorer's first slide was of a sailboat. Finder explained that the floor of a boat or ship is called a **deck**. The front of a boat is called the **bow**. As you look forward, the right side of a boat is the **starboard** side. One picture showed the boat sailing far out to sea.

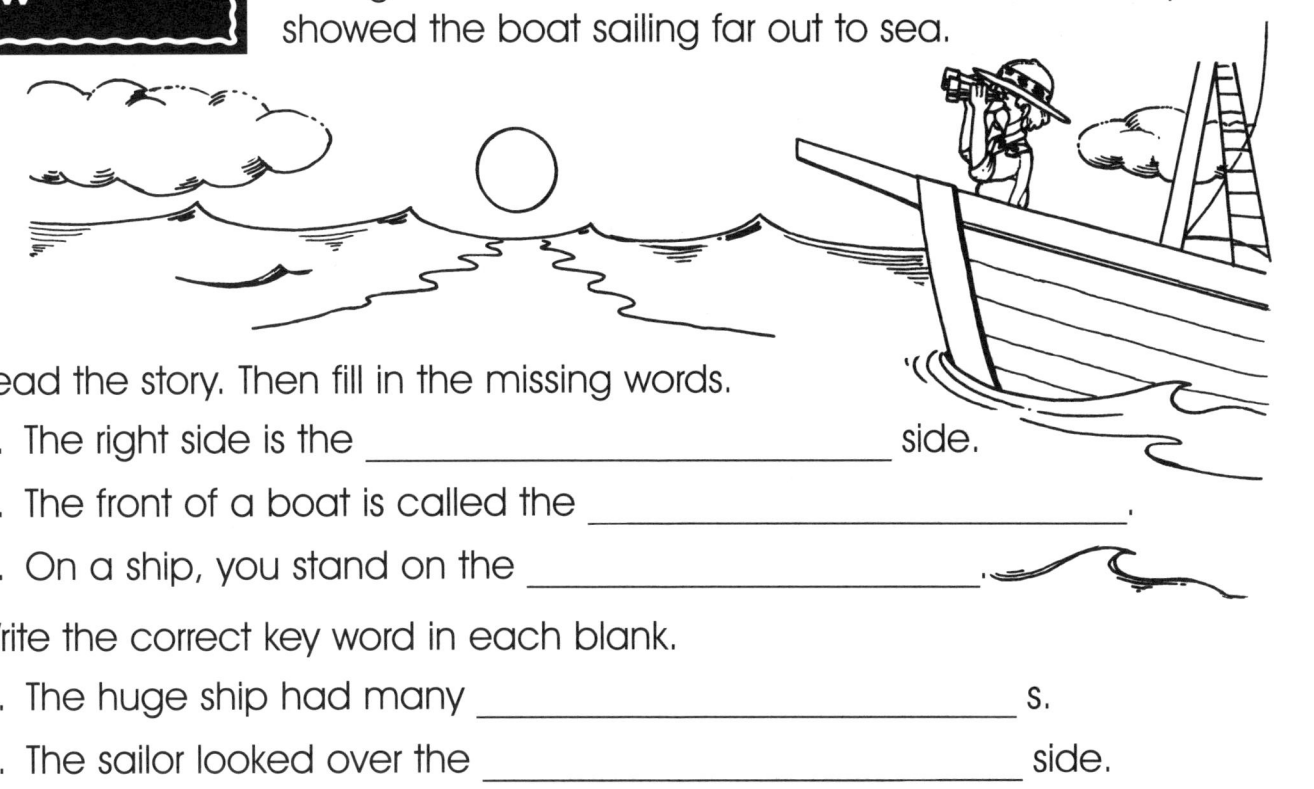

A. Read the story. Then fill in the missing words.

1. The right side is the _____ side.

2. The front of a boat is called the _____.

3. On a ship, you stand on the _____.

B. Write the correct key word in each blank.

1. The huge ship had many _____ s.

2. The sailor looked over the _____ side.

3. They stood looking ahead from the _____ of the ship.

C. The words **deck** and **bow** have more than one meaning. Match the right meaning with its sentence.

1. **deck**   a. floor of ship    b. pack of playing cards

   Marco played with the deck. _____

   The explorer paced the deck. _____

2. **bow**   a. front of ship    b. to bend at waist

   Rachel stood at the bow. _____

   You will bow to Queen Anne. _____

On another sheet of paper, draw a picture of a ship. Label the **starboard, deck,** and **bow.** Then write a sentence using each key word. Use both meanings of **deck** and **bow.**

Name_____ Date_____

# Key Words

**expedition
voyage
safari**

Long ago, Bill Finder had heard tales of a strange animal that lived on Hidden Island. A few years ago, he began to plan an **expedition** to find it. When he was ready, his **voyage** to the island took nine days. After he reached the shore, Finder and his helpers organized a **safari**, or hunting party, to find the wild, unknown beast.

A. Read the story. Then fill in the missing words.

   1. The _____ took nine days.

   2. A hunting party is called a _____.

   3. The _____ was planned to look for a strange animal.

B. Write the correct key word in each blank.

   1. The travelers' _____ led them to another country.

   2. The members of the _____ traveled through the jungle looking for animals.

   3. Columbus' _____ sailed west to find a way to China.

C. Fill in the puzzle using the key words.

   1. trip from place to place
   2. trip with a purpose
   3. trip to hunt for animals

If you could go on an expedition anywhere in the world, where would you go? Write a story about your adventures in this place.

MP5095 - Reading and Writing                            Reading Comprehension

Name_____    Date_____

# Key Words

trench
moat
furrows

The group set off on their safari. Soon one of the hunters saw small ditches in the ground. Finder studied them.

"These are **furrows**," he said. "They were made by a plow. That means there are people on the island."

The afternoon of the same day, the group came to a wide, deep ditch. Finder explained that it looked like a **trench**. He guessed that someone might have dug it to hide people during a battle. Further on, the hunters came to a fort with a **moat** around it. The deep, water-filled canal made it hard to get into the fort unless the bridge was down.

A. Read the story. Then fill in the missing words.

1. The _____ was to protect the fort.
2. _____ are made by a plow.
3. The _____ might have hid people during a battle.

B. Write the correct key word in each blank.

1. A narrow ditch made by a plow is a _____.
2. A deep ditch filled with water is a _____.
3. A long ditch used in battle is a _____.

C. Unscramble the words. Use the symbols to read the hidden message.

n  e  c  r  h  t       o  m  t  a       s  r  o  w  f  u  r

MP5095 - Reading and Writing                21                Reading Comprehension

# Key Words

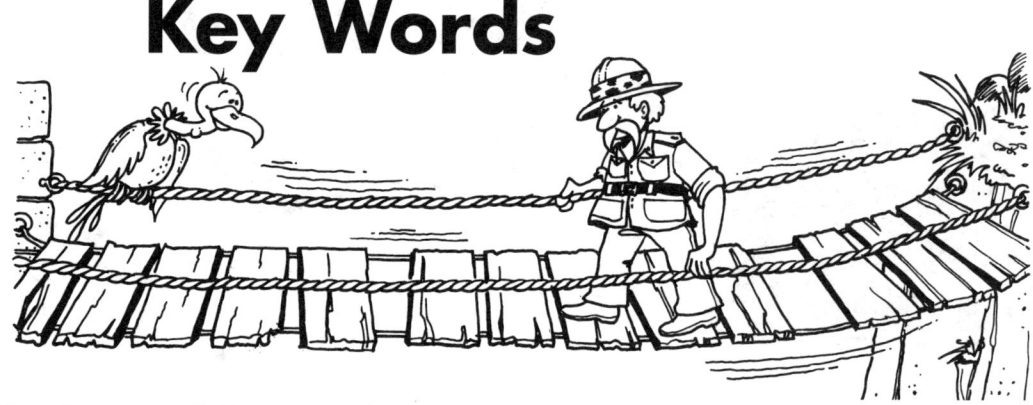

**calamity**
**trouble**
**misfortune**

The explorers walked around the moat. When they reached the back of the fort, they saw an old bridge. Bill Finder hurried ahead to test it.

He called to the others, "Watch your step, there are boards missing. Try to avoid **trouble**." The rotting bridge squeaked and swayed as the group crossed. One of the sailors tripped, but others caught him before he fell. The sailor took a deep breath.

"Tripping is only a **misfortune**. Falling into the dark, dirty water of that moat could be a real **calamity**!"

A. Read the story. Then fill in the missing words.

1. One sailor had the _____ to trip.
2. Falling into the moat would be a _____.
3. Watch where you are going to avoid _____.

B. Write the correct key word in each blank.

1. He had the _____ to fall downstairs.
2. If you talk in school, you may get in _____.
3. When the roof fell in, it was a _____.

C. What kind of event is each of the following? Circle each calamity. Underline each misfortune. Put an ! after anything that would cause trouble.

1. earthquake
2. hitting someone
3. losing your money
4. bad snowstorm
5. being unlucky
6. playing a prank

Find a story in the newspaper about a calamity or misfortune. On another sheet of paper, write what you might do if you were there.

Name_____ Date_____

# Key Words

realized
achieve
execute

The group spent a day exploring the empty fort. Some people wanted to stay longer, but all wanted most to **achieve** the goal of the expedition. As leader, Finder broke the group into two parties. Each group had special tasks to **execute**, or carry out.

For three more days, the two parties pushed deeper into the island's woods. At last, they found the strange animal. They had **realized** the purpose of their safari.

A. Read the story. Then fill in the missing words.

 1. Each group had special tasks to _____.

 2. The explorers wanted to _____ their goal.

 3. Finding the strange animal _____ the purpose of the trip.

B. Write the correct key word in each blank.

 1. When you finish a task, it is _____.

 2. If you reach your goal, you _____ it.

 3. When you carry out orders, you _____ them.

C. The word **realized** has more than one meaning. Match the right meaning with its sentence.

 a. understood     b. accomplished

 1. _____ After much hard work, Tina **realized** her goal to earn $10.

 2. _____ Spencer **realized** that it takes effort to earn money.

Write about three things that you have accomplished this year. Then write about three things you still want to achieve.

MP5095 - Reading and Writing       23       Reading Comprehension

# Key Words

summary
digest
brief

As Finder told about finding the strange animal, the audience sat on the edge of their chairs. When the explorer finished, they applauded and called for more. Finder laughed.

"As you leave the auditorium, you will each get a booklet. It is a **digest**, or short report of the trip with descriptions of the animal and other things we found. There is a **summary** at the end to give you a **brief** overview. This will help you to recall the main events. Thank you. You have been a great audience."

A. Read the story. Then fill in the missing words.
   1. A _____ is a short report.
   2. The _____ was at the end of the book.
   3. The summary was _____.

B. Write the correct key word in each blank.
   1. Adam gave a _____ report about rabbits.
   2. For your book report, you could write a _____.
   3. Becky read the original book, but I read the _____ of it.

C. The words **digest** and **brief** have more than one meaning. Match the right meaning with its sentence.

   **brief**   a. using few words        b. for a short time
   1. We made a **brief** stop at the store. _____
   2. The mayor had a **brief** statement for us. _____

   **digest**   a. a short form        b. to absorb food
   3. The explorer, Bill Finder, gave us a **digest** about his trip. _____
   4. Mother said, "Chew slowly, so you can **digest** your food." _____

Pretend you were on Finder's expedition. What do you imagine the strange animal looked like? On another sheet of paper, draw its picture and write a brief summary of your findings about the animal.

Name_____ Date_____

# Review

| | | | |
|---|---|---|---|
| audience | furrows | safari | expedition |
| calamity | audio | deck | realized |
| voyage | summary | bow | auditorium |
| trench | execute | digest | misfortune |
| trouble | achieve | moat | starboard |
| brief | | | |

A. Use words from the box to fill in the blanks.

1. The _____ was to see a special program.
2. The girl was standing on the _____ of the ship.
3. The _____ took nine days.
4. The _____ was to find the strange animal.
5. One person had the _____ to trip.
6. The explorers wanted to _____ their goal.
7. A short book is a _____.

B. Choose the correct word from the box.

1. The _____ part is the sound part.
2. The right side of a ship is called the _____ side.
3. A trip for a special purpose is an _____.
4. A long ditch used in battle is a _____.
5. An event of great loss is a _____.
6. When you complete a task, you have _____ it.
7. A review of the main ideas is a _____.

Name _____ Date _____

# Key Words

**sustain
maintain
prolong**

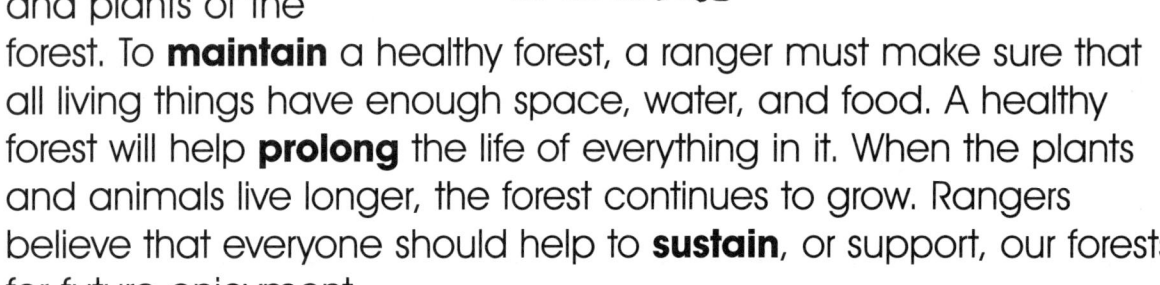

Forest rangers watch over the animals and plants of the forest. To **maintain** a healthy forest, a ranger must make sure that all living things have enough space, water, and food. A healthy forest will help **prolong** the life of everything in it. When the plants and animals live longer, the forest continues to grow. Rangers believe that everyone should help to **sustain**, or support, our forests for future enjoyment.

A. Read the story. Then fill in the missing words.

 1. Everyone should help _____ our forests.

 2. A forest ranger's job is to _____ a healthy forest.

 3. Care will help _____ the life of the forest.

B. Write the correct key word in each blank.

 1. People want to _____ their lives.

 2. She wanted to _____ good health, so she ate the right foods.

 3. A snack will _____ us until lunch.

C. Use the key words to fill in the puzzle.

 1. to keep growing

 2. to take care of

 3. to make last longer

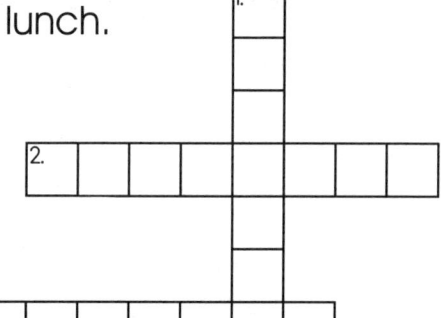

On another sheet of paper, make a list of five things you can do to help maintain your health.

# Key Words

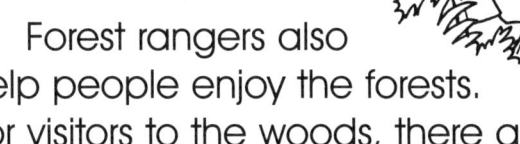

**toddlers**
**youth**
**adult**

Forest rangers also help people enjoy the forests. For visitors to the woods, there are three programs that explain how to maintain the forest. For the **toddlers**, who are very young children, rangers have short walks with baby animals to see and touch. For the **youth**, the older children, the pace is faster. The trail is longer. The points of interest include many kinds of plants and animals. The special **adult** program gives many ways to help maintain and sustain life in the forest.

A. Read the story. Then fill in the missing words.

1. The _____ saw the baby animals.
2. The _____ saw many plants and animals.
3. The _____ program told how to maintain and sustain the forest.

B. Write the correct key word in each blank.

1. The _____ was two years old.
2. You can vote when you become an _____.
3. The teenagers belonged to a _____ club.

C. Draw lines to match each key word with two things that a person in that stage might do.

1. be a teacher          **toddler**      4. go to high school
2. be a scout member     **adult**        5. sit in a high chair
3. ride a tricycle       **youth**        6. drive a taxi

Name _____  Date _____

# Key Words

**pebbles**
**boulder**
**gravel**

One interesting trip is the journey to White River. Here, the ranger points out the huge **boulder** at the top of the waterfall. The water falls over this enormous rock to the river below. The ranger always stops at a little pool near the waterfall. The water is very clear and the **pebbles** on the bottom are full of color. The little rocks are very smooth because they have tumbled around in the water, rubbing against each other over and over. At the edge of the river is a **gravel** beach made of small, gray rocks.

A. Read the story. Then fill in the missing words.
  1. The waterfall came over the _____.
  2. The _____ are full of color under water.
  3. The beach was made of _____.

B. Write the correct key word in each blank.
  1. He skipped _____ across the water.
  2. They drove up the _____ driveway.
  3. A huge _____ blocked the trail.

C. Unscramble these key words.
  1. b e p l e b s
     _ _ _ _ _ _ _
     ◧ ■ □ □ ▼ ■ ◉

  2. o l e b u r d
     _ _ _ _ _ _ _
     □ ⊠ ▽ ▼ ■ ■ ◐

  3. a l g v r e
     _ _ _ _ _ _
     o ◐ □ ▽ ■ ▼

  4. Write the hidden message. Use the code from your unscrambled words.

  _ _ _ _ _ _   _ _ _ _ _   _ _ _   _ _ _ _ _
  ◧ ■ ⊠ ◧ ▼ ■   ▽ □ ▼ ▼ ■   ⊠ ▽ ◐   w ⊠ ◐ ▼ ■

Name _____ Date _____

# Key Words

**fragrance**
**aroma**
**scent**

Forest rangers also plan walks along wooded trails. Along the edge of one trail, you can see many wild flowers. If you stop, you can smell the sweet **fragrance**. When you walk through the pine trees, you sniff a new **aroma**. The smell reminds one of Christmas and its many spicy odors. At one spot, the ranger points to a leafy plant and asks you to sniff the air. Here, the **scent** is awful! The forest ranger laughs and tells us that this plant is called a skunk cabbage. One sniff and you have to agree. The skunk cabbage has the right name.

A. Read the story. Then fill in the missing words.

   1. The wild flowers had a sweet _____.

   2. The skunk cabbage had an awful _____.

   3. Pine trees have an _____ of their own.

B. Write the correct key word in each blank.

   1. The spicy _____ of gingerbread filled the air.

   2. The perfume has a sweet _____.

   3. The dog followed the _____ of the rabbit tracks.

C. Use the key words to fill in the puzzle.

   1. spicy odor
   2. stinky smell
   3. sweet smell

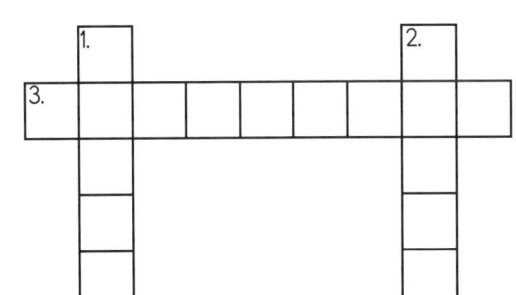

Describe your favorite smell in a few sentences. What smell did you choose? Why is it your favorite?

MP5095 - Reading and Writing     Reading Comprehension

Name_____ Date _____

# Key Words

lichen
moss
ferns

    Down another trail, our ranger pointed to a pale, flat plant clinging to a large boulder. She told us that what we saw was really two plants growing together. It is called **lichen**. The paired plant grows slowly on both rocks and trees. Next, the ranger pointed to a soft, green pad spreading over the ground. She said that this was **moss**. It is made up of many tiny plants. Among the trees were plants that look like large, green feathers. The ranger called these **ferns**. We learned that the forest is home to many wonderful plants.

A. Read the story. Then fill in the missing words.

   1. Two plants growing together make _____.

   2. Leafy plants that look like feathers are _____.

   3. Many small plants growing together like a soft pad are _____.

B. Write the correct key word in each blank.

   1. Kenny touched the soft pad of _____ on the tree.

   2. Many people grow _____ as houseplants.

   3. Rocks in the forest are often covered with _____.

C. The forest ranger pointed out three types of plants. List these in the order she showed them to us.

_____

_____

_____

Choose one of the three kinds of plants above. Read more about the plant in an encyclopedia or other resource. Write three important facts about the plant you chose.

Name_____ Date_____

# Key Words

**disclose**
**exposed**
**display**

Below one large tree grew a thick clump of ferns. Our ranger pulled back the ferns to **disclose** tree roots. These roots could be seen easily because they were **exposed** and lying above ground. Water had washed away the soil. Among the roots was a hidden nest. Later, at the museum, we saw a fine **display** and many special exhibits about the animals and plants living in the forest.

A. Read the story. Then fill in the missing words.

1. There was a fine _____ at the museum.

2. The roots could be seen because they were _____.

3. The ranger pulled back the ferns to _____ the roots.

B. Write the correct key word in each blank.

1. I will _____ the secret tomorrow.

2. The museum had an interesting rock _____.

3. The secret agent _____ the spy plot.

C. Put the following words in alphabetical order.

| lichen | disclose | aroma | scent |
| moss | ferns | display | exposed |

_____     _____
_____     _____
_____     _____
_____     _____

Create your own story about a spy. Write about your spy's adventures on another sheet of paper.

Name_____ Date_____

# Key Words

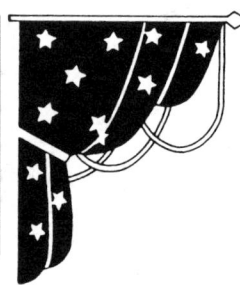
liberated
justice
freedom

The people of the United States are very proud of their free nation. Americans have many symbols which show this pride in **freedom**. The Liberty Bell was rung when the country was **liberated**, or freed, from English rule. The symbol of the Liberty Bell reminds people of this special event. Another symbol that Americans use is a balance scale. Courts of law use this symbol to show that they try to be fair to everyone. They want **justice** for all people.

A. Read the story. Then fill in the missing words.

1. Courts want _____ for all people.

2. The Liberty Bell was rung when America was _____.

3. Many symbols show Americans' pride in _____.

B. Write the correct key word in each blank.

1. The guilty person was brought to _____.

2. The captured people were finally _____.

3. You have the _____ to choose how you will live.

C. Unscramble the words. Then use the symbols to read the hidden message.

s c u i e j t            b a d i r t e l e            e e m f o r d

___ ___ ___ ___ ___ ___ ___    ___ ___ ___ ___ ___ ___ ___ ___ ___    ___ ___ ___ ___ ___ ___ ___
▲ ▽ ⊖ △ • ⊗ ■              ▼ • □ ■ ◐ □ △ ■ ■             ○ ◑ ■ ■ ■ ⊠ ▽

___ ___ ___ ___ ___ ___ ___       ___ ___ ___       ___ ___ ___
▼ • □ ■ ◐ △ y              ○ ⊠ ◐         □ ▼ ▼

Choose one of the United States and write a paragraph about it. Use books and other resources to help you find information.

MP5095 - Reading and Writing     32     Reading Comprehension

# Review

| | | | |
|---|---|---|---|
| boulder | lichen | disclose | aroma |
| toddlers | pebbles | sustain | youth |
| fragrance | display | prolong | adult |
| liberated | justice | ferns | moss |
| freedom | maintain | gravel | scent |
| exposed | | | |

A. Use words from the box to fill in the blanks.

1. Forest rangers help to _____ the forest.
2. The walk for _____ lets them see baby animals.
3. The waterfall came over the _____.
4. Pine trees have an _____ of their own.
5. Many small plants growing like a soft pad are _____.
6. The roots could be seen because they were _____.
7. A court tries to achieve _____ for all people.

B. Write the correct word from the box in each blank.

1. To keep something going, you must _____ it.
2. An older child is a _____.
3. Smooth, round rocks are _____.
4. A sweet smell is called a _____.
5. A grown-up person is an _____.
6. To tell about something is to _____ it.
7. To be set free is to be _____.

MP5095 - Reading and Writing   33   Reading Comprehension

# Key Words

**gloomy**
**cheerful**
**dreary**

It was a **gloomy** day. The sky was overcast. It was cloudy and rainy. Sam gazed out the window and complained, "What a dull, **dreary** day!" Usually, Sam was a **cheerful**, happy person.

"The trouble with a rainy day is that there is nothing to do," sighed Sam. Then he had a good thought. "I'll take my new book and read in a cozy corner with a bright light."

A. Read the story. Then fill in the missing words.

1. What a dull, _____ day!

2. It was a _____ day.

3. Usually, Sam was a _____ person.

B. Write the correct key word in each blank.

1. It was a dark and _____ time.

2. The weather was _____

3. Her smile showed how _____ she felt.

C. Put the words under the correct heading.

| sad | happy | dismal | merry | frown |
| jolly | dreary | smile | grin | pout |

1. cheerful      2. gloomy

_____     _____

_____     _____

_____     _____

_____     _____

_____     _____

What do you like to do on gloomy, dreary days? Write a few sentences on another sheet of paper.

Name _____  Date _____

# Key Words

**recipe**
**formula**
**prescription**

Sam sat down and opened his book. To his surprise, a folded paper fell into his lap. On the paper, strange markings were printed in red ink. Maybe it was something written in a code. At the top, Sam read, "4 U."

Before he started to work on the code, Sam wondered, "Was the note a **recipe** with a list of food and seasonings to make something to eat? Were the symbols part of a **formula** telling how to put together something new? Or, was the message like a **prescription** written by a doctor? Hmm, what could it be?"

A. Read the story. Then fill in the missing words.

   1. Was it a _____ to put together something new?

   2. Was this a _____ to make something to eat?

   3. Was this a _____ from a doctor?

B. Write the correct key word in each blank.

   1. The doctor gave me a _____ for my cold.

   2. The scientists worked out a _____ for a special plastic.

   3. The cook used a new _____.

C. Use the key words to fill in the puzzle.

   1. cook's plan

   2. secret recipe

   3. doctor's order

Make a list of ingredients from your favorite recipe. What would happen if you left out the main ingredient? Write a sentence on how you think this new food would taste.

Name _____ Date _____

# Key Words

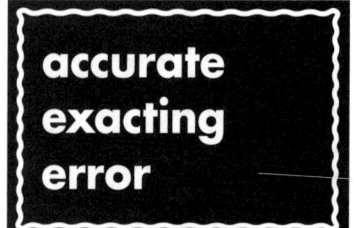

**accurate
exacting
error**

Sam really enjoyed puzzles. Could he read these symbols quickly, or would he make an **error**? He must make no mistakes. He would need to be very **accurate**. Sam counted each number and letter. He found that some symbols were used over and over. Sam set to work in an **exacting** way. In an hour, he had cracked the code!

A. Read the story. Then fill in the missing words.

1. He would need to be very _____.

2. Sam set to work in an _____ way.

3. He did not want to make an _____.

B. Write the correct key word in each blank.

1. I made an _____ on my math test.

2. John hung his clothes in the closet in an _____ way.

3. You must be _____ when you do math.

C. Unscramble the words. Then use the symbols under the words to write the hidden message.

c a a u t c r e        o r e r r        e i a c t x n g

☐ ⊗ ⊗ ▽ ◐ ☐ ▲ ■    ■ ◐ ◐ ⊠ ◐    ■ ◗ ☐ ⊗ ▲ • ▲ o

___ ___ ___ ___ ___ ___ ___ ___ ___ ___ ___ ___

•    ⊗ ☐ ▲    ⊗ ◐ ☐ ⊗ k    ⊠ ▽ ◐    ⊗ ⊠ d ■

Think of a time that you had to solve a problem. Write a story about the problem and the steps you took to solve it.

MP5095 - Reading and Writing       Reading Comprehension

# Key Words

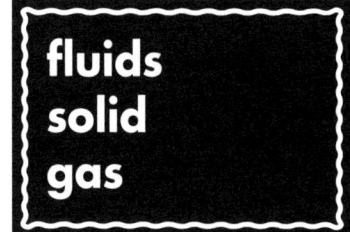

fluids
solid
gas

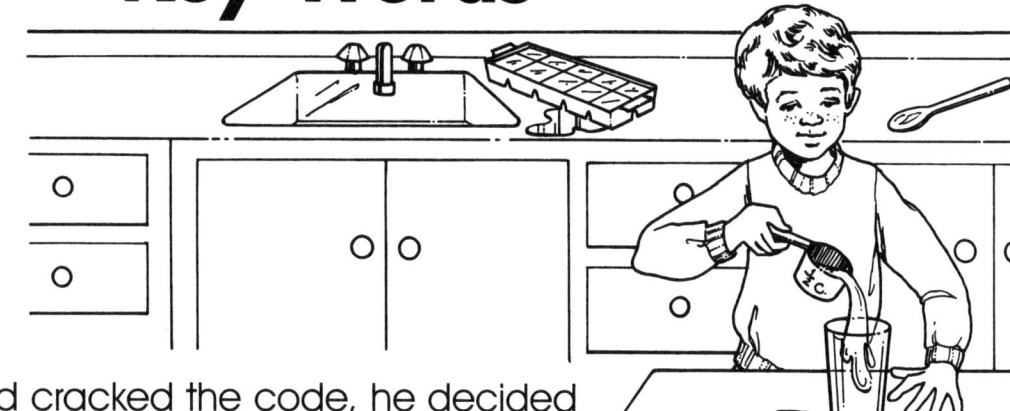

Now that Sam had cracked the code, he decided to follow the directions in the message. He read, "Get three kinds of things that do not hold their shape." So, Sam got three **fluids**. He poured a cup of water, a half cup of orange juice, and a half cup of lemon juice into a glass. Next, Sam read, "Get six things that are **solid**, but will make steam with the others." Sam added six ice cubes. Then, Sam looked at his mixture. The sudden cold made steam rise. "Hmm," said Sam, "this rising mist is a vapor. Like our air, it is a **gas**."

A. Read the story. Then fill in the missing words.

1. Sam called the vapor a _____.

2. Sam got three kinds of _____.

3. He got six _____ things.

B. Write the correct key word in each blank.

1. Objects such as wood that hold their shape are _____s.

2. Rising air is a _____.

3. Things that flow are _____.

C. Use the key words to fill in the puzzle.

1. will flow
2. becomes a vapor
3. holds shape

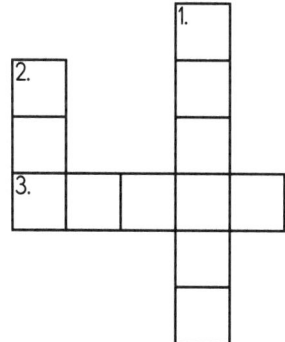

**Solids, fluids** (liquids), and **gases** are called states of matter. Give an example of an item in each state of matter.

Name _____ Date _____

# Key Words

**nutritious**
**inhale**
**wholesome**

Sam held the steaming glass and gazed at the light orange fluid. He put the glass to his nose to **inhale** its smell. It had the fragrance of fresh oranges. Sam thought about the fluid mixture he had made. Fruit juices are **nutritious**. They help you to grow. This fluid was very **wholesome**. Drinking it would help to maintain his good health.

A. Read the story. Then fill in the missing words.

1. Fruit juice is _____.
2. Sam wanted to _____ the fragrance of the oranges.
3. The fluid was very _____.

B. Write the correct key word in each blank.

1. They will _____ the aroma of the food.
2. She lived in a _____ environment.
3. Your diet should be _____ if you are to grow.

C. Write the key words in alphabetical order.

_____
_____
_____

Plan a nutritious breakfast, lunch, and dinner. Use the key words in a paragraph about the meals you have created.

# Key Words

**responsible**
**certain**
**negligent**

At last, Sam returned to the cozy corner and his book. He took a sip of the nutritious fluid. He was **certain** that it was safe to drink. He knew that he had been very **responsible** in following the directions. Sam wondered who had put the message into the book. The message could have been carried out in a dangerous way. Was someone **negligent** or careless to leave such a message for anyone to find?

A. Read the story. Then fill in the missing words.

1. Sam had been very _____.

2. Was it _____ to leave such a message?

3. When Sam drank the fluid, he was _____ that it was safe.

B. Write the correct key word in each blank.

1. Parents are _____ for their children's actions.

2. If you don't take care of your pet, you are _____.

3. Jackie was _____ that she could do the problem without making an error.

C. Use the key words to fill in the puzzle.

1. being sure

2. to be accountable for your actions

3. to be careless

**EXTRA!** Think of a job you might want to have someday and write it on another sheet of paper. Under the name, list five responsibilities of a person in the job you have chosen.

# Review

| | | | |
|---|---|---|---|
| prescription | wholesome | error | inhale |
| responsible | accurate | gloomy | dreary |
| negligent | cheerful | recipe | gas |
| exacting | certain | solid | fluids |
| nutritious | formula | | |

A. Use words from the box to fill in the blanks.

1. Usually Sam was sunny and _____.
2. Was the message a _____ to create something new?
3. Sam worked on the code in an _____ way.
4. Sam needed six things that were _____.
5. He held the glass to his nose to _____ it.
6. When Sam drank the fluid, he was _____ that it was safe.

B. Write the correct words from the box in the blanks.

1. An overcast sky seems _____.
2. A list for making something to eat is a _____.
3. Not to make a mistake is to be _____.
4. Things that flow are _____.
5. Food that helps you to grow is _____.
6. A person who can account for his actions is _____.

Name _____  Date _____

# Review

C. Write a word from the box on page 40 that is the opposite of each word listed.

1. cheerful _____
2. error _____
3. fluid _____
4. responsible _____

D. Use the words from the box on page 40 to fill in the puzzle.

**Across**

4. helps you grow
6. food formula
9. things that flow
10. vapor
12. doctor's formula
14. careful
15. dull day

**Down**

1. breath in
2. mistake
3. careless
5. holds shape
6. accounts for actions
7. happy
8. overcast
11. correct
13. to be sure

MP5095 - Reading and Writing  41  Reading Comprehension

# No Sugar?

Aaron's class learned about making healthy choices. They studied the food pyramid. They learned to read labels on food products.

After school, Aaron stopped at a store for a snack. He wanted something sweet, but he remembered what his teacher had said about eating too much sugar. Carefully he read labels before making his choice.

"Look, Mom," he said proudly. "I bought this snack because there's no sugar listed on the label. It tastes good too."

"Glucose, sucrose, lactose, and fructose," Aaron's mother read. "Corn syrup and honey. I'm glad you read the label first, but I guess there's one thing your teacher forgot to tell you."

"What's that?" Aaron asked.

"Glucose, sucrose, lactose, and fructose are other names for sugar."

"Oh," said Aaron. "No wonder it tasted so good."

1. Number the sentences in the order in which they occur in the story.

    ____ Aaron read the label before he bought his snack.

    ____ Aaron's mother said that sugar has other names.

    ____ Aaron's class learned about eating healthy.

2. What are other names for sugar? _____
   _____

3. What do you think Aaron told his class the next day?
   _____
   _____

Name_____  Date _____

# What's Your Birthstone?

People have been making and wearing jewelry since the Stone Age. Necklaces of animal teeth and bones were worn to scare away evil spirits. Later, people wore rare or valuable stones to bring good luck, health, and happiness.

Many years ago, a different stone with a special meaning became connected with each month of the year. In the 16th century, people began wearing jewelry with the special stone for the month when they were born. They called these birthstones.

| Month | Color | Birthstone | Symbolizes |
|---|---|---|---|
| January | deep red | garnet | constancy |
| February | violet | amethyst | sincerity |
| March | sea-blue | aquamarine | courage |
| April | clear | diamond | innocence |
| May | bright green | emerald | love, success |
| June | white | pearl | health, longevity |
| July | bright red | ruby | contentment |
| August | light green | peridot | married happiness |
| September | bright blue | sapphire | clear thinking |
| October | various | opal | hope |
| November | gold | topaz | fidelity |
| December | sky blue | turquoise | prosperity |

Today people do not believe wearing birthstones will bring good luck, happiness, or health, but they still enjoy wearing birthstone jewelry.

1. What is the main idea of this article?

    A. Birthstones bring good luck.
    B. People like to wear jewelry.
    C. People have worn birthstones for hundreds of years.

2. Which three birthstones are shades of blue? _____

_____

3. How are the January and July birthstones similar?

_____

4. When did people first start wearing birthstones? _____

5. What is your birthstone? _____

# The Trolls of Scandinavia

Trolls are creatures found in stories told in the Scandinavian countries of Sweden, Denmark, Norway, Iceland, and nearby islands. They are short with wrinkled faces, gray skin and hair. Some male trolls have long beards. Trolls are very strong for their size.

Trolls have long noses so they can smell danger from far away. Their large, furry ears help them hear wolves. With their wide, flat feet, they can walk through deep snow. Their thick, leathery skin protects them from harsh weather and insect bites. They use their long tails to tickle other trolls.

Trolls have small eyes and poor eyesight. "He couldn't tell a tree from a hole in the ground" is a favorite troll saying.

1. Name four Scandinavian countries. _____
   _____

2. Why do trolls have:

   wide, flat feet _____
   _____

   large, furry ears _____
   _____

   thick, leathery skin _____
   _____

   long noses _____
   _____

Name _____ Date _____

# Imagine Eating 500 Pounds of Food a Day!

Read the article about elephants. Then answer the questions.

Elephants are the largest land animals. Male elephants can be 9 to 11 feet tall and weigh 10,000 to 15,000 pounds. Even baby elephants weigh more than many people. Can you imagine a 200 pound newborn baby?

An elephant's trunk is very powerful. It can lift, carry, and pull objects as heavy as a tree trunk. Yet, an elephant can pick up an object as small as a peanut with its trunk. In hot weather, an elephant cools itself by spraying water on its back. The long, flexible trunk is really part of the elephant's upper lip, as well as its nose.

An elephant's tusks are really teeth that have grown very long. Most elephants have two tusks which can weigh 50 to 100 pounds. Many elephants have been killed for their valuable ivory tusks. Poachers ignore laws that protect elephants from hunters.

Elephants are vegetarians. They eat grass, leaves, bamboo shoots, fruit, and tree bark. An adult elephant can consume nearly 500 pounds of food a day! Can you imagine eating that much?

1. What is the author's purpose for writing "Imagine Eating 500 Pounds Of Food a Day!"?

    A. To relay information to the reader

    B. To entertain the reader

    C. To persuade the reader to believe what he or she believes

2. List five facts you learned about elephants.

    _____
    _____
    _____
    _____
    _____

Name _____ Date _____

# African and Asian Elephants

Have you ever noticed that some elephants have much smaller ears than others? These elephants originally came from Asia. The ones with the larger ears came from Africa. Their ears may be two-and-a-half to three-and-a-half feet across. There is another unusual thing about African elephants: they always sleep standing up.

Study the pictures of the African and Asian elephants. Then put an X in the correct column.

Asian Elephant              African Elephant

|  | Asian | African | Both |
|---|---|---|---|
| Has tusks |  |  |  |
| Has two fingerlike extensions on end of trunk |  |  |  |
| Has one fingerlike extensions on end of trunk |  |  |  |
| Has larger ears |  |  |  |
| Has smoother forehead |  |  |  |
| Has two humps on forehead |  |  |  |
| Has looser, more wrinkled skin |  |  |  |
| Is smaller |  |  |  |

# Monumental Monuments

The Washington Monument stands in Washington, D.C. in honor of our first president, George Washington. Workers began building the Washington Monument in 1848. It took 40 years to complete the brick and concrete structure. At that time, the 555-foot memorial was the tallest monument in the world.

Visitors can take an elevator or walk the 898 steps to the top of the monument. Windows facing all four directions provide a terrific view of the city.

The Statue of Liberty stands on a small island in New York Harbor. It symbolizes our country and the freedoms people enjoy. The statue has a steel frame with a copper covering. The 151 foot statue contains 100 tons of copper and 125 tons of steel.

The Statue of Liberty was a gift from the people of France. To ship it to the United States, it had to be taken apart and sent by ship in 214 huge crates. America received the pieces in 1885. During the following year, the statue was erected on a 65-foot base and an 89-foot stand.

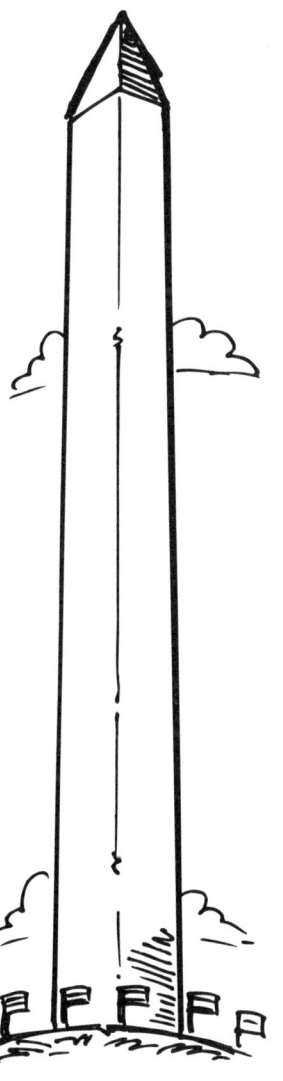

Complete the chart.

|  | **Washington Monument** | **Statue of Liberty** |
|---|---|---|
| Location |  |  |
| Height |  |  |
| Material Made of |  |  |
| Year Completed |  |  |

Pretend you need to create a monument to honor your hero. Write a paragraph about your hero to put on the monument. Then draw a picture of your monument.

# Hurray for the Red, White, and Blue!

The red, white, and blue flag of the United States of America stands for its people and their government.

The first official U.S. flag had 13 stars and 13 stripes. The flag today has 50 stars!

Today's flag still has the same number of stripes as the first flag, reminding us of the first 13 colonies that became states.

Many people call our flag the "Stars and Stripes" or "Old Glory."

Compare the first U.S. flag with the current one.

| Questions: | The first U.S. flag | Today's U.S. flag |
|---|---|---|
| How many stars? | | |
| How many stripes? | | |
| What color? | | |
| What do the stars stand for? | | |
| What do the stripes stand for? | | |
| What do the colors stand for? | | |

Name _____   Date _____

# Devan's Letter

833 Newbury Street
Ripon, Wisconsin 54971
September 10

Dear Grandpa and Grandma,
I really like our new house. We have four bedrooms. One for me, one for Tori, and one for Mom and Dad. You can sleep in the other one when you come visit. Dad said we can get a dog next week. Tori wants a poodle so she can dress it up in doll clothes. I think we should get a beagle.
I started at Lincoln School last week and already made two new friends, Joel and Jon. My teacher is Mr. Mandenheimer, but we call him Mr. M. for short.
We have a big back yard. My friends and I play football.
Write back. I miss you and all my friends in Arizona.

love,
Devan

Who wrote this letter? _____

What is the main idea? _____
_____
_____

MP5095 - Reading and Writing    49    Reading Comprehension

# Cause and Effect

Draw lines to connect the sentences that tell what happened and why.

 Josh ran a two-mile race.

Josh taught his puppy a new trick.

 Josh and his puppy went for a walk in the woods.

Josh played basketball in the house.

Josh studied hard for his spelling test.

 The first time Josh played the violin, the sound was terrible.

The lamp fell off the table and broke.

His puppy howled when he heard the noise.

He got a good grade on his test.

His puppy chased a squirrel.

His puppy rolled over.

He was very thirsty.

# Alligators and Crocodiles

Alligators and crocodiles are reptiles. They both have tough skin and bony plates of armor. They eat insects, fish, and small animals by crushing their prey in their strong jaws.

When a crocodile closes its jaws, two large teeth show on each side of its mouth. An alligator's teeth do not show when its mouth is closed.

Notice how their eyes and noses are on the tops of their heads. This lets alligators and crocodiles see and breathe while hiding and swimming low in the water.

Mother crocodiles and alligators build nests of sand and leaves on land. Babies hatch from the eggs.

Alligators have shorter, rounded snouts. The crocodile's snout is long and pointed. Its skin is greener than an alligator's and it grows a little larger.

Put an X in the correct columns.

|  | Alligators | Crocodiles | Both |
|---|---|---|---|
| They lay eggs. |  |  |  |
| They always have two teeth showing |  |  |  |
| They are reptiles. |  |  |  |
| They grow larger. |  |  |  |
| They have shorter, rounded snouts. |  |  |  |
| Their eyes and noses are on the tops of their heads. |  |  |  |

# A Mixed-Up Story

Number the sentences in order to make sense of the story. Use a pencil so you can erase if needed.

A. _____ She carried a knapsack of goodies for her grandmother.

B. _____ Finally she met three billy goats.

C. _____ Snow White told them she wanted to visit her grandmother in Brooklyn, but was lost.

D. _____ "I think you're in the wrong story," said the first billy goat.

E. _____ "If I can," the first billy goat replied.

F. _____ "Can you help me? she asked.

G. _____ Then she started off again.

H. _____ "Of course," said the second billy goat.

I. _____ Along the way, she got lost.

J. _____ "You can't get there from here," said the second billy goat.

K. _____ She went home and changed her name to Little Red Riding Hood.

L. _____ "Well, maybe," answered the third billy goat.

M. _____ What was she to do?

N. _____ Once upon a time, Snow White set off to visit her sick grandmother.

O. _____ "I think you need to start this story over," said the third billy goat.

P. _____ After she heard their advice, Snow White knew just what to do.

# Pecos Bill—A Tall Tale Hero

People enjoy hearing and telling tall tales—stories about people who have great adventures and can do amazing deeds. Sometimes the stories are based on a real person or a true event, but in a tall tale, the truth gets stretched.

When Pecos Bill was a toddler, his family decided to move West because they had too many neighbors. The closest one was only 50 miles away—much too close for comfort.

His parents loaded everything into a covered wagon along with their 18 children. As they crossed the Pecos River, the wheel hit a rock and little Bill bounced out of the wagon.

No one noticed he was missing until it was too late. An old coyote found Bill and adopted him. Since no one knew his real name, he became Pecos Bill.

The coyotes took good care of Bill and taught him everything they knew. He grew healthy and strong.

One day, as Pecos Bill ran through the desert, he met a cowboy named Chuck. "How come you're running around like a coyote?" Chuck asked.

"Because I am a coyote," Bill replied.

"Horsefeathers!" Chuck answered. "If you are a coyote, where is your long bushy tail?"

Chuck led Pecos Bill to a river where he could see his reflection. Bill was amazed. Chuck was right. He didn't have a long, bushy tail. He wasn't a coyote after all.

1. How did Pecos Bill get his name? _____
   _____

2. How did Bill discover he wasn't a coyote? _____
   _____

Name _____ Date _____

# The Secret of Alexandria Elementary School

    Alec the Elephant lived in the Alexandria Elementary School. No one knew he lived there except Mr. Grey, the custodian, and he didn't mind at all. Sometimes Mr. Grey got lonely at night and Alec was good company.

    During the day, Alec stayed behind the furnace in the basement and kept very quiet. He was cozy and warm in the winter and pleasantly cool in the summer. Once the children left for the day, Alec was free to roam the halls.

    Alec spent an hour or two in the gym, doing exercises so he wouldn't get too fat. When Mr. Grey took his break, the two of them shared a bag of peanuts and a bottle of root beer.

    Each evening Alec checked out all the classrooms. He squeezed into the first grade classroom to see the newest pictures the children had drawn. Once he tried to fit into a desk, but that was a disaster. He got stuck and had to wait an hour before Mr. Grey came by to get him unstuck.

    Alec lumbered down the hall to read the poems and stories hanging on the walls in Mr. B.'s second grade class. He usually stopped and straightened up Suzie's desk while he was there. She always forgot before she went home.

    He visited the four bunnies in the third grade classroom and the two snakes who lived in glass cages. Alec figured the snakes must be smarter than the rabbits, because they were in fourth grade.

1. What was the "secret" of Alexandria Elementary School?
   _____

2. Who knew Alec lived there? _____

3. List three interesting things Alec might see if he visited your classroom.
   _____
   _____
   _____

4. Could this be a true story? _____
   Why or why not? _____
   _____

Name_____     Date _____

# The Turtle Goes to War

    Submarines are not modern inventions. The first submarine used in war was the Turtle, a one-person sub invented by David Bushnell. He planned to use it against British warships during the Revolutionary War.

    The British used their warships to form a blockade in New York Harbor in 1776. They wouldn't let any American ships leave or enter the harbor with goods or supplies.

    The Turtle was only seven-and-a-half feet long and six feet wide. The submarine was shaped like an egg and made of oak with bands of iron.

    The Turtle had no means of propulsion. The only way to move the submarine under water was for the person inside to turn a crank by hand to move the propeller.

    The submarine also had no air supply. The submarine had to return to the surface within 30 minutes or the operator ran out of air.

    To make the submarine sink, the operator opened a valve to admit seawater into a ballast tank. The seawater made the submarine too heavy to float. To make the submarine rise, he emptied the tank with a hand pump.

1. Blockade means _____
2. Propulsion means _____
3. Ballast means _____

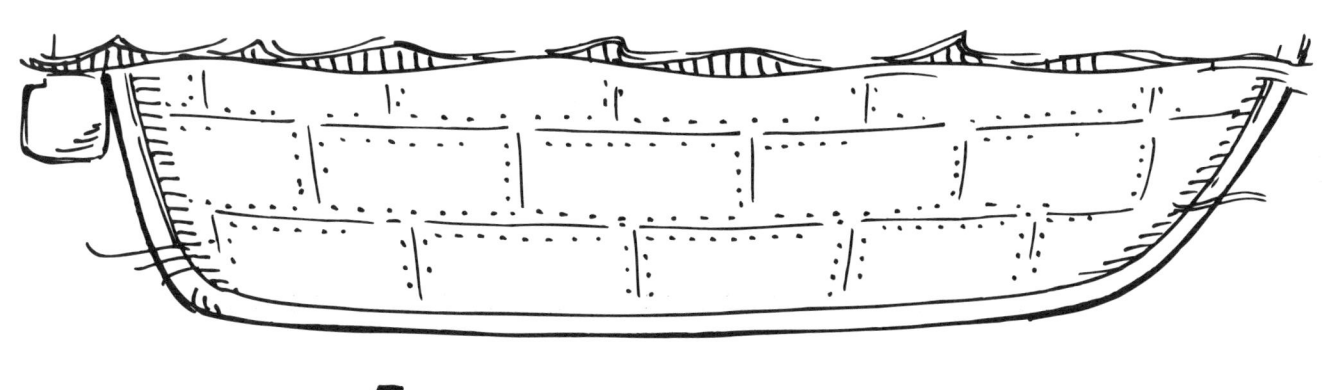

# Yellowstone Vacation

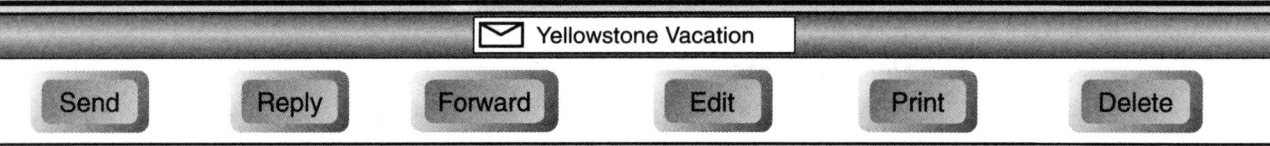

From: Kate@email.com
To: Uncle Joe; Grandpa B; Mary S; Jim C: Bonnie H; Jerry
Sent: June 24
Subject: Yellowstone Vacation

Dear Friends and Family,

I had such a great time on my vacation to Yellowstone National Park I wanted to share the experience with you. I'll have photos on my website in the next few days so you can check those out.

I started my tour of the park by driving the 140 mile Great Loop Road that makes a huge figure eight through the park. One of the first signs I saw said DO NOT FEED THE BEARS. That one had me worried all week.

I did see a few bears, but I stayed in the car with the windows rolled up. I didn't bother them and they didn't bother me. I also saw bison, big horn sheep, and many smaller animals. I learned from a ranger that there are more than 300 types of animals that live in Yellowstone. Wait until you see that photo I took of the herd of elk!

Although it's late June, many mountains still had snow. Some of the peaks are nearly 8,000 feet high.

I also saw the Liberty Cap, an extinct hot spring. Other hot springs are still active. The most spectacular was Mammoth Hot Spring, a 300-foot waterfall! I was so excited about writing to you, I haven't even unpacked yet. I'll do that now and write more tomorrow.

love,
Kate

1. Why did Kate write this letter? _____

2. What kinds of animals did she see? _____

3. Why was there still snow on the mountains in June? _____

# Making Candles

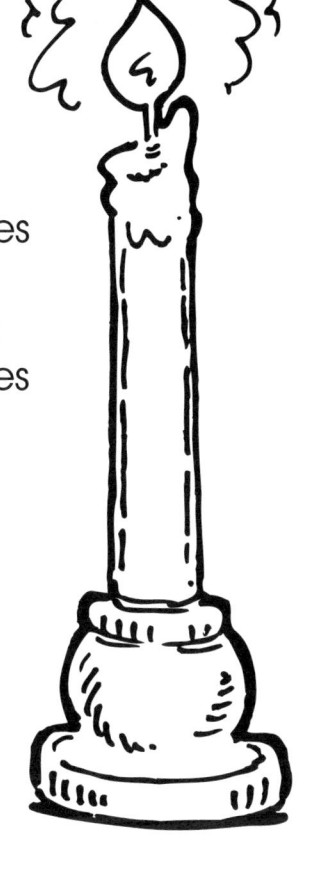

Before they had electricity, people relied on firelight, candles, torches, and lanterns as sources of light.

Candles were made by dipping a wick made of flax or cotton fibers into melted wax or fat. The hot wax adhered to the wick and became hard when it cooled. Candles were made thicker by dipping them into the melted wax several times and allowing the wax to cool and harden each time.

Herbs, spices, or dried flower petals were added to the wax or fat to make candles smell better. The most expensive candles were made from bee's wax.

Jack be nimble, Jack be quick
Jack jumped over the candlesticks.

This nursery rhyme is based on a game children played while their parents made candles. After dipping candles, people hung them from two long horizontal sticks while they hardened and cooled. These sticks, and not the candles themselves, were the "candle sticks" Jack jumped over.

1. List light sources people used before they had electricity.
   _____
   _____

2. List light sources we use now.
   _____
   _____

3. Do you think the people making candles liked children to play this game? Why or why not?
   _____
   _____

# The Legend of King Arthur

According to legends told in England, Uther Pendragon was the King of England. His son, Arthur, was born about 500 A.D. The king's magician, Merlin, predicted the king would soon become ill and die. The king's enemies would try to kill the baby to keep him from becoming king.

King Uther believed Merlin and asked him to protect Arthur until he was old enough to take his place on the throne. Merlin secretly gave the baby prince to Sir Ector to raise as his own son.

As Merlin had predicted, King Uther soon died. For the next 18 years, Britain had no king. Lords and barons raised private armies and fought each other.

Finally the Archbishop of Canterbury asked Merlin for advice about how Britain could find a king who could unite the people and bring peace. Merlin devised a plan. He promised that soon a descendant of King Uther would take his rightful place on the throne.

Knowing that a large tournament would soon be held in London, Merlin used his magic to place a sword up to its hilt in an anvil on a stone. The golden hilt was encrusted with gems.

Knights from all over England arrived to test their abilities with sword and spear. Among them were Sir Ector and his two sons, Sir Kay and Arthur. Merlin announced that whoever could pull the sword from the anvil would become the rightful King of Britain.

1. Why did King Uther allow Merlin to take his baby son?
   _____

2. Underline what happened first.
   a. King Uther died
   b. Merlin gave the baby to Sir Ector.

3. Underline what happened last.
   a. Sir Ector and his sons arrived at the tournament.
   b. Merlin placed a sword in an anvil.

4. What does "encrusted" mean? _____

5. What does "devised" mean? _____

Name _____  Date _____

# One Hump or Two?

Camels are large mammals native to desert regions of Asia and Africa. The Arabian camel, also called a dromedary, has one hump. The Bactrian camel has two humps. Camels can go several days without food or water. Food, not water, is stored in their humps.

When food is plentiful, camels' humps swell and become firm. When food is scarce, the humps shrink and become soft as the camels use up their supplies of stored fat.

Camels are well adapted for desert conditions including infrequent supplies of food and water, blazing heat during the day, low temperatures at night, high winds, and blowing sand. Camels have wide feet with pads that keep them from sinking into the sand as they walk.

Their long eyelashes protect their eyes from blowing sand. Camels can also close their nostrils during a windstorm. Their sharp teeth allow them to bite off and chew tough thorny plants. Their long necks help them reach leaves on trees. They can reach down to drink water and eat grass without having to bend their legs.

1. What is the main idea of this article?
   ____ Bactrian camels have two humps.
   ____ Camels are well suited to desert life.
   ____ There are two kinds of camels.

2. Why don't camels sink into the sand when they walk?
   _____

3. What is the purpose of a camel's hump?
   _____

Arabian camels, native to northern Africa, are called dromedaries, and have one hump.

Bactrian camels, native to Asia, have two humps.

Name _____  Date _____

# Om-pah, Om-pah Booms the Tuba

**tuba**

Do you like the sounds of a marching band? Have you ever heard a concert by an orchestra? Many types of instruments combine to make music fun and interesting to hear.

There are four basic types of instruments: strings, woodwinds, brass, and percussion.

The shiny brass instruments are an important part of every band and orchestra. As the name implies, they are made of metal. Sound is produced by blowing into a mouthpiece.

**trumpet**

To produce notes on a trombone, the musician moves a slide back and forth. Valves on a trumpet, cornet, French horn, saxhorn, and tuba can be opened and closed in different combinations to produce notes.

**trombone**

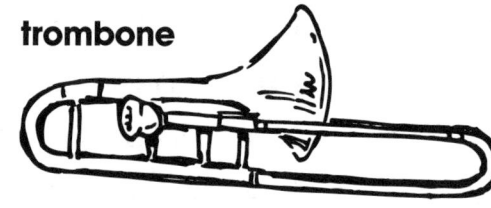

The tuba produces the lowest, deepest sounds. A French horn's mellow tones blend well with the strings and woodwinds.

1. What are the four basic types of instruments?

   _____

   _____

2. How do musicians produce sound on brass instruments?

   _____

   _____

3. Which brass instrument does not use valves to produce notes?

   _____

4. Which brass instrument produces the lowest, deepest notes?

   _____

**saxhorn**

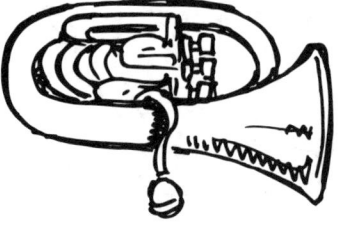

**cornet**

**French horn**

Name _____   Date _____

# The Strings Sing

Stringed instruments are usually made of wood. The violin, viola, cello, and bass are played with a bow. The musician rubs the bow across the four strings to create music. By pressing strings in different places, different notes are produced.

Guitars, banjos, mandolins, and ukuleles have between four and eight strings, depending on the type. Musicians use either their fingers or a plectrum to pluck the strings. A plectrum is a small piece of wood, metal, ivory, or plastic.

Musicians have played harps for nearly 5,000 years. Made of wood, these stringed instruments come in many shapes and sizes. The modern harp used in an orchestra is quite large and has 46 strings.

Put an X on the line to show how sounds and notes are produced on brass and stringed instruments.

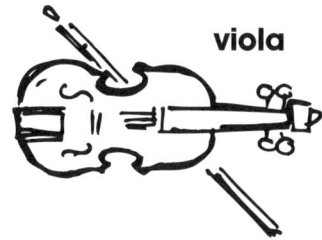
bass

viola

mandolin

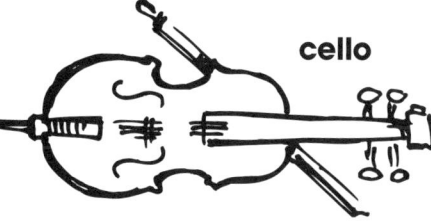
violin   guitar

cello

|   | Brass | Strings |   |
|---|-------|---------|---|
| 1. | ____ | ____ | With a bow |
| 2. | ____ | ____ | By blowing |
| 3. | ____ | ____ | By moving a slide |
| 4. | ____ | ____ | By opening and closing valves |
| 5. | ____ | ____ | By plucking |

List the stringed instruments by type.

| Stringed instruments played with a bow | Stringed instruments that are plucked |
|---|---|
| _____ | _____ |
| _____ | _____ |
| _____ | _____ |
| _____ | _____ |

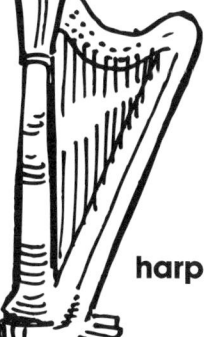
ukulele

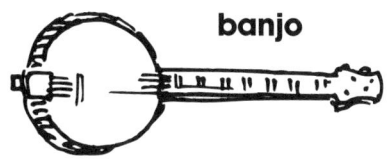
banjo

harp

MP5095 - Reading and Writing        61        Reading Comprehension

# Listen to the Flute

The piccolo, flute, oboe, bassoon, clarinet, saxophone, and English horn are woodwind instruments. At one time, all woodwind instruments were made of wood. Today, some, like the piccolo, flute, and saxophone, are usually made of metal.

Sound is produced by blowing air into a hole or over a vibrating reed. Musicians use their fingers to open and close holes in the instruments to produce different notes.

The piccolo, the smallest of the woodwinds, makes high, shrill sounds. The bassoon produces low, deep sounds.

1. At one time, all woodwind instruments were made of _____.

2. Today, some woodwinds, like the _____ _____, and _____ may be made of metal.

3. Describe how musicians produce sound and different notes on woodwinds.
   _____
   _____
   _____

4. List three ways woodwinds are different from stringed instruments.
   _____
   _____
   _____

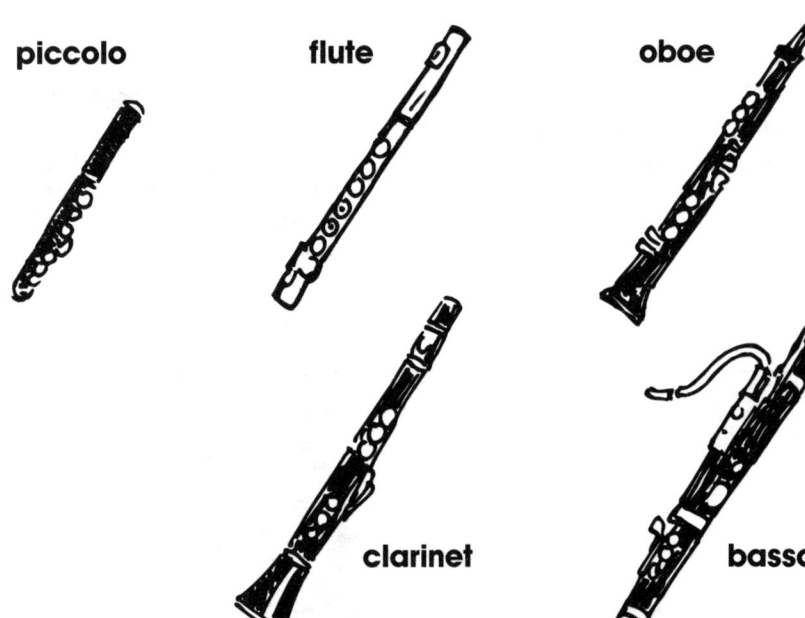

Name_____    Date _____

# Boom, Boom, Boom

Bands and orchestras use many types of percussion instruments. They are either shaken or struck to produce sound.

**tambourine**

**kettle**

The earliest type of percussion instruments may have been hollow logs. Using sticks, musicians could produce a deep, steady beat for singers and dancers.

Musicians use special wooden sticks or metal brushes to play snare drums, bass drums, and kettle drums. Bass drums produce the lowest, deepest sounds.

**bass**

**maracas**

Other percussion instruments include the xylophone, triangle, gong, bells, cymbals, maracas, and tambourine. Sometimes even blocks of wood are clicked together or struck with drumsticks to produce specific types of sounds.

**snare**

**cymbals**

List three examples for each type of instrument. (see pages 60-62 for help)

**bells**

### Brass
_____
_____
_____

### Strings
_____
_____
_____

**gong**

### Woodwinds
_____
_____
_____

### Percussion
_____
_____
_____

**xylophone**

**triangle**

What is your favorite instrument? Write a few sentences explaining why you like it best.

MP5095 - Reading and Writing          63          Reading Comprehension

# Belling the Cat

Long ago a group of mice lived in the same house with a very watchful cat. The mice were constantly in danger.

One day they held a meeting to discuss what to do about the cat. Many mice talked about the problem, but none had any ideas about what to do.

Finally, one of the smallest mice spoke up. "We all agree that the cat can sneak up on us too easily. If we could hear her coming, we would have time to run to safety. I think we should put a bell around the cat's neck. Then we will always know when she is near."

The other mice cheered. They congratulated the smallest mouse on his marvelous idea. Finally, their problem was solved.

Then the oldest mouse spoke. "Belling the cat is indeed a grand idea, but who will do it?"

Not one mouse spoke.

1. What is the moral of this fable?

    ____ Cats are sneaky.

    ____ Proposing a plan is easier than putting it into action.

    ____ Warning bells are good protection for mice.

2. What do you think the mice did next?

    _____

    _____

3. Imagine you are one of the mice. Propose another solution.

Name _____  Date _____

# Crazy Compound Words

When two smaller words are put together to form a new word, the new word is called a compound word. For example, when dog and house are joined, the word doghouse is formed.

Form three new compound words by joining one word from Row A with one from Row B. After the word, write its definition.

| Row A: | butter | tooth | basket | pan | night |
|---|---|---|---|---|---|
| Row B: | chair | fish | house | man | boat |

New words and definitions.

1. _____

2. _____

3. _____

Name_____    Date_____

# Homophones: Same Sound, Different Spellings and Meanings

steak–stake
hair–hare
mail–male
waste–waist
son–sun

Words that sound alike but are spelled differently and have different meanings are called **homophones**. These words make a picture in your mind. If you think of the wrong meaning, you will get a funny picture.

A. Write the homophone that makes the sentence correct.

1. Mother fixed a _____ for dinner.

2. His head was covered with _____.

3. She put the _____ into the box.

4. Jo put a belt around her _____.

5. The _____ was shining in the sky.

B. Write the correct word in each blank.

1. **steak stake**  We bought _____ at the store. The _____ was in the ground.

2. **hair hare**  A _____ is very much like a rabbit. Please comb your _____!

3. **mail male**  A letter came in the _____. The opposite of female is _____.

4. **waste waist**  Empty the _____ basket. A belt goes around your _____.

5. **son sun**  The _____ shines brightly. Father said, "Tom is my _____."

Draw a picture that shows one set of homophones. For example, you could draw a man carrying some letters to show **male** and **mail**.

MP5095 - Reading and Writing

Name_____ Date_____

# Homophones: Same Sound, Different Words

Words that sound alike but are spelled differently and have different meanings are called **homophones**. These words can make a funny picture in your mind if you use the wrong one.

Read the meaning of each word carefully. Write the correct words in the blanks.

**cent**—a coin, often called a penny
**scent**—a smell or an odor
**sent**—to cause to go

1. I _____ a letter to my friend.
2. The candy cost one _____.
3. The _____ of roses filled the air.
4. Bob _____ many _____ for the _____ ed flower.

**do**—to make, perform, or complete
**dew**—tiny drops of water, moisture
**due**—something owed, time to bring in, or pay

5. My library book was _____.
6. Can you _____ it?
7. The _____ was on the grass.
8. _____ you see the _____ spots on the book that is _____?

**foul**—something nasty or gone wrong
**fowl**—a bird of any kind

9. Many kinds of _____ were in the barnyard.
10. The _____ ball went out of bounds.
11. The scent of the dead _____ was _____.

Write a paragraph using the homophones **cent**, **scent**, and **sent**. Be sure to use each word correctly!

Name _____ Date _____

# Homographs: Same Sound, Different Meanings

Some words can be used in many ways. The story on this page will show you four ways to use the key word.

Moe, Joe, and Sloe were three snakes. They lived under the **shed** in the backyard. Their home was full of tools and mice. The snakes craved mice to eat. The three snakes grew so big that they began to **shed** their skins. Young snakes lose their skins more often than old ones.

Sloe was cold so he started a fire. At first the fire glowed and **shed** light all around.

Moe said, "It is getting smokey in here."

Joe said, "Yes, the smoke hurts my eyes." Before long, the smoke made all of them cry and **shed** tears.

A. Read the story. Then fill in the missing words.

1. If you cry, you _____ tears.
2. Snakes _____ their skins as they grow.
3. You can keep tools in a _____.
4. A fire glows and _____ light.

B. On another paper, write a sentence for each of the four ways to use the word **shed**.

1. a building
2. to make flow (as tears)
3. to give off light
4. to lose hair or skin

C. Match the meaning with the sentence.

_____ 1. cry           a. The dog shed its hair.
_____ 2. building      b. The lamp shed its light on us.
_____ 3. lose hair     c. baby shed tears.
_____ 4. give light    d. The shed was full of tools.

# Another Homograph

Matt, the curious mouse, weighed himself on the **scale**. His weight was one-half pound. "I am too thin," said Matt. To get more food, he had to climb the wall. He learned to **scale** the wall quickly.

One day, he saw Mrs. White cleaning fish. She scraped one **scale** after another from the fish.

Mrs. White called to her child Sally, "Don't forget to play your **scale** on the piano."

"How curious!" said Matt. "So many ways to use one word."

A. Read the story. Then fill in the missing words.

1. The fish had shiny _____s.

2. Matt weighed himself on the _____.

3. Sally played a _____ on the piano.

4. Matt could _____ the wall quickly.

B. On another paper, write a sentence for each of the four ways to use the word **scale**.

1. climb a mountain        3. a thing for weighing
2. snake or fish skin      4. piano notes

C. Match the meaning with the right sentence.

_____ 1. piano     a. The snake was covered with scales.
_____ 2. climb     b. She played the scale well.
_____ 3. weigh     c. We will scale the mountain.
_____ 4. skin      d. Please step on the scale.

Name_____  Date _____

# Figures of Speech

An old story says that long ago Johnny Appleseed went all over the American countryside planting apple trees. Even though the story may not be true, nutritious apples seem to be a very American fruit. People have many sayings using the word **apple** in different ways. A word or phrase used in a special way is called a **figure of speech**. Watch for colorful ways of saying things. Unusual phrases can make reading and speaking more fun!

A. Read these figures of speech. Can you add to the list?

1. You're the **apple of my eye**.—my favorite
2. There's **always a bad apple in every barrel**.—in any group of things, some will be less than good.
3. That's **as American as apple pie**.—anything common and popular in the United States
4. She was an **apple-cheeked** child.—round and rosy cheeks
5. He's an **apple polisher**.—flatterer, one who shines the apple to make it look better than it is
6. **An apple a day keeps the doctor away**.—Regular use of something good makes for health.

B. Write the figure of speech that fits each sentence.

1. She is my best girl.

   _____

2. Try to keep from becoming sick.

   _____

3. Everybody uses these sayings.

   _____

4. In a crowd, some strangers could be bad.

   _____

Write two figures of speech that you have heard. Write what each figure of speech really means.

MP5095 - Reading and Writing

Name _____ Date _____

# Writing Sentences

Write two things you would do . . .

if you landed on a new planet.
First,
_____
_____

Second,
_____
_____

if you went on a hot air balloon ride.
First,
_____
_____

Second,
_____
_____

if you were as small as Tom Thumb.
First,
_____
_____

Second,
_____
_____

Name _____  Date _____

# Brainstorming and Topic Sentences

Complete questions **1** and **2** before writing the story about the zoo.

1. What have you seen at a zoo that is . . .

   green? _____  orange? _____
   red? _____  brown? _____
   yellow? _____  white? _____

2. What zoo things go with these words?

   furry? _____  tiny? _____
   fluffy? _____  huge? _____
   cuddly? _____  friendly? _____

Write two sentences to tell about the **topic sentence** below.

A trip to the zoo is fun for two reasons.
   First, _____
   _____
   _____
   _____

   Second, _____
   _____
   _____
   _____

MP5095 - Reading and Writing     Writing

Name _____  Date _____

# Topic Sentences

The topics listed below are ideas for paragraphs. Turn these ideas into complete sentences. Write a complete topic sentence for each topic below.

**Example:**   Topic: (Riding the bus)
Topic sentence: My brother and I like to ride the bus when we go to visit our grandfather.

1. Topic: (Snow). Topic sentence: _____
_____

2. Topic: (Going shopping). Topic Sentence: _____
_____

3. Topic: (A favorite meal). Topic sentence: _____
_____

4. Topic: (Spare time). Topic sentence: _____
_____

5. Topic: (Favorite shoes). Topic sentence: _____
_____

6. Topic: (Friends). Topic sentence: _____
_____

7. Topic: (Chores at home). Topic sentence: _____
_____

Select one of your topic sentences. Develop it into a full paragraph. Begin with the topic sentence. Then, write four or more complete sentences about your topic.

_____
_____
_____
_____
_____

Name_____  Date_____

# Paragraphs and Topic Sentences

Write two sentences to tell about the **topic sentence** below.

Word List:

| science | art | teacher | sports | reading | math |
| music | gym | friends | homework | principal | bus |

At school there are two things that I do well.

First,

_____

_____

_____

★ _____

_____

_____

Second,

_____

_____

_____

★ _____

_____

_____

At the star, give a reason why you do each thing well. Begin your sentence after the ★.

Name _____   Date _____

# Paragraphs and Topic Sentences

Write two sentences to tell about the **topic sentence** below.

Word List:

| rocket | explore | stars | blast-off | launch | universe |
|--------|---------|-------|-----------|--------|----------|
| orbit | spacesuit | astronaut | moon | weightless | planet |

I'd like to travel in space for two reasons:

First,

_____

_____

_____

✶ _____

_____

_____

Second,

_____

_____

_____

✶ _____

_____

_____

Explain each reason further. Begin your sentence after the ✶.

Name _____  Date _____

# Happy Holidays

Write a topic sentence that states the main idea for each story.

_____
_____
_____

After dad cut off the top, I took out the squishy middle part. Then I drew a face on the pumpkin. Dad cut out the eyes, nose, and mouth. On Halloween, we put a candle inside and lit it. We had the best jack-o-lantern of all!

_____
_____
_____

We watched the parade in the morning. Then we had a picnic and played baseball. When it was dark, we watched the fireworks explode in the sky. It's the only holiday in the middle of summer!

_____
_____
_____

Molly cut hearts from red and pink paper. She added glitter and stickers. Then she wrote a special message on each one. Everyone thought Molly's hearts were beautiful.

Name _____ Date _____

# Recognizing Paragraphs

You may have noticed that **paragraphs** are frequently **indented**. That is, the first line begins to the right of the margin by about a four letter space.

Below is a group of words about lions. The words tell three main ideas, so there should be three paragraphs. Read through the words. Decide where sentences begin and end. Decide where the paragraphs begin and end. Cross out any sentences that do not tell about the main ideas of the paragraphs. Circle the beginning word of each paragraph. Put a capital letter at the beginning of each sentence. Put a period at the end of each sentence.

**Most wild lions live in Africa the king of beasts, as it is called, prefers grass covered plains there its sandy coloring blends perfectly with the ground and the sun-burned grass lions seldom wander into heavy forests, and they avoid deserts because of the scarce food supply lions are carnivorous this means that they eat other animals for food lions hunt for animals like the antelope, the zebra, and the bush pig lions adapt easily to living in zoos very old lions live on smaller animals like rodents a lion fears only three animals they are the full-grown buffalo, elephant, and rhinoceros the rhino has a short, broad head and a single horn he knows that these animals are much stronger than he is if it came to a fight, the lion would lose**

What is the main idea of each paragraph about lions?

1. _____
2. _____
3. _____

Write a paragraph of your own beginning with this main idea: On the way home from school yesterday, I saw a strange light glowing in the sky.

_____
_____
_____
_____
_____
_____
_____
_____

Name _____  Date _____

# Telling an Experience

When writing paragraphs, try to make your beginning sentence interesting. A good beginning makes your reader want to keep on reading.

The following paragraph needs a beginning. Read the paragraph. Then write a good beginning of one or two sentences.

_____
_____

*My homework was difficult. I worked on it a long time and finished it right before I ate dinner. After eating, I returned to my room. To my horror, I discovered that my dog had torn my papers to bits.*

Write a paragraph telling about something you did or about something that happened to you. Here are some possible topics to use.

**Topics:**
- Something you did that made you feel good
- A time you were frightened (or happy, or sad)
- A time you got lost
- Something funny that happened last week
- Something you lost (found, hid)

Choose a topic for your paragraph, then write a good beginning sentence below.

_____
_____

Plan the details of your paragraph. Write these on the lines below. You do not need to write complete sentences.

_____
_____
_____
_____

Now write your paragraph on another sheet of paper. Use your beginning sentence and details from above. Express the details in complete sentences.

Name_____    Date _____

# Celebrations!

All over the world, people celebrate special occasions. Birthdays, Christmas, Hanukkah, Kwanzaa, and Independence Day are a few such occasions.

Think about one holiday that you celebrate with your family. Then answer the questions below.

1. What is the name of the holiday?
   _____
   _____

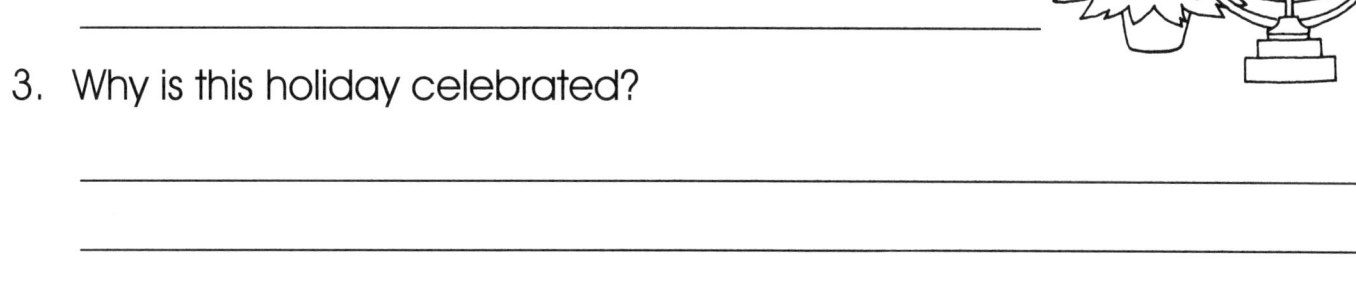

2. When do you celebrate this holiday?
   _____
   _____

3. Why is this holiday celebrated?
   _____
   _____
   _____
   _____

4. How do you celebrate this holiday?
   _____
   _____
   _____
   _____
   _____

Write a paragraph about your favorite holiday memory. Why is this memory so special to you?

Name _____  Date _____

# Summarizing a Book

Often when you read a book, you will be asked to write about it. You need to include the important facts that are important to the story.

Choose a book that you think you will like. Read the book. Then fill out the report below.

Title: _____

Author: _____  Illustrator: _____

Characters in the Story: _____

Problem or Conflict in the Story: _____

The Solution: _____

Name_____    Date_____

# Using Headlines

    Headlines in newspapers are meant to attract the attention of readers. They are usually short, to the point, and in larger print than the articles themselves.

    Find two headlines in your local newspaper that sound interesting. Cut them out. Glue one headline below and the other on another sheet of paper. Without reading the articles, write what you believe the articles are about. Then read each article and write a brief summary. Were your predictions right?

1. Glue the first headline here.

2. Write what you believe the article is about.

   _____

   _____

   _____

3. Read the article and write a brief summary.

   _____

   _____

   _____

   _____

   _____

   _____

   _____

Name_____   Date _____

# A House Is a Home

You have decided to enter the "Design Your Dream House Contest." What will your home look like? How big will it be? What will the outside look like? How many rooms will the house have? Be as creative and original as possible.

Answer the questions below.

1. How would your new house be different from where you live now?

   _____
   _____
   _____
   _____

2. What strange and exciting things would you put in your house that most houses do not have?

   _____
   _____
   _____
   _____

3. Which room would be your favorite? Why?

   _____
   _____
   _____
   _____

 On another sheet of paper, draw a picture of your dream house. Write a few sentences describing its features.

# Island Paradise

You have the chance to travel to a tiny, deserted tropical island with one other person. A small boat will take you to the island and drop you off. You will be staying on the island for a month before the boat returns to take you home. Since the boat is small, you can take only a few items with you. Plenty of food will be on the island.

1. If you could take only three items, what would they be? Why?

   _____
   _____
   _____

2. How could you use the island's natural resources?

   _____
   _____
   _____

3. Who would you most like to join you on this trip? Why?

   _____
   _____
   _____

 When people travel they often keep a journal to remember their trip. On another paper, write a journal entry for one day and night on the island.

# Friends Are Forever

Friends are people with whom we share things, go places, and do things. Being a good friend is hard work.

Think about a good friend of yours. Use the letters of the alphabet to write 26 words or phrases to describe this person and why he or she is such a good friend.

Example:   Always there for me
Best friend
Caring person

When you finish, share your work with your friend, or write your phrases on a blank greeting card to give to your friend on a special occasion.

A _____
B _____
C _____
D _____
E _____
F _____
G _____
H _____
I _____
J _____
K _____
L _____
M _____

N _____
O _____
P _____
Q _____
R _____
S _____
T _____
U _____
V _____
W _____
X _____
Y _____
Z _____

Name _____  Date _____

# Keeping a List

People write lists to help them remember things like phone numbers of friends and relatives, grocery items needed, or things to do.

Sometimes the list needs to be written in a specific order. Think about tomorrow. What kinds of things do you have planned? Make a list of what you will do tomorrow or what you would like to get done. Write the list in order. For instance, the first one might be to wake up at 7:30 a.m. Try to be as accurate as possible. Save the list until tomorrow. Then keep it with you all day. As you complete each item, cross off that number. Did you accomplish all that you thought you would?

My List of Things to Do

1. _____
2. _____
3. _____
4. _____
5. _____
6. _____
7. _____
8. _____
9. _____
10. _____
11. _____
12. _____
13. _____
14. _____

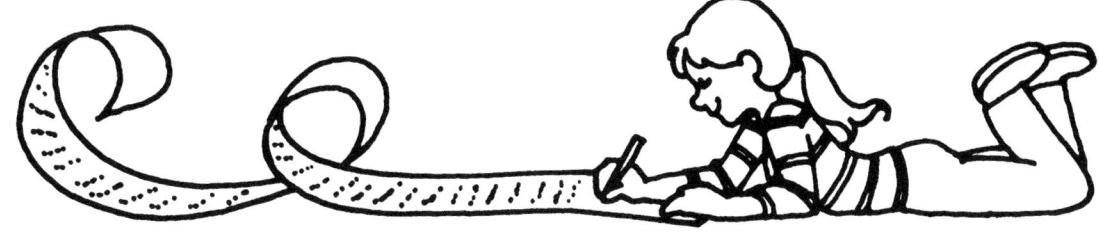

Name _____  Date _____

# Fame and Glory

There are many great and famous people: presidents, kings, queens, scientists, authors, artists, athletes, and others. If you could meet any one of these people, living or dead, whom would you most like to meet? Think about this person for a while, and then answer the questions below.

1. Whom would you most like to meet? Why?

   _____
   _____

2. What does or did this person do to become famous?

   _____
   _____
   _____

3. How did this person change or affect the world?

   _____
   _____
   _____
   _____

4. What, if any, are the characteristics of this person that you share?

   _____
   _____
   _____

MP5095 - Reading and Writing          Writing

Name_____  Date _____

# A Personal Letter

**Heading**

2784 Lattice Road
Tucson, AZ 85702
October 10, 2002

**Writer's address**
Street
City, state, zip code
month, day, year

**Greeting**

Dear Larry,

**Body**

At last we are settled in our new home. Putting everything into a new place took a lot of work. I'm glad it's finally done.

I've made some nice new friends, but it takes time to feel close to people. I still miss you and my other friends in Chicago.

My school is very different from the one I had before. This school is all on one floor. It seems as if you walk for miles to get from one place to another.

I hope you can visit me sometime. I'd like to show you around. You would enjoy the desert and the mountains.

**Closing**
**Signature**

Your friend,
Rick

Notice the Super Commas, above. What rules can you make for using commas in a letter? (Of course, you should use regular commas when you write.)

**Rule 1:** A comma is used in the date between the _____ and the _____.

**Rule 2:** In the second line of the heading, a comma is used to separate the _____ and the _____.

**Rule 3:** Two parts of a letter that end with a comma are the _____ and the _____.

Notice where the heading, closing, and signature are placed on the paper. Make a rule about this.

**Rule 4:** The heading, closing, and signature are placed _____
What part of the letter lines up along the edge? _____
Do the beginning words of the greeting and closing start with capital letters? _____
Does the second word in the closing also have a capital letter? _____

Write a letter to an imaginary pen pal in another country.

Name _____    Date _____

# Writing a Description

When you tell about something, you describe it. You use words that help your reader get a picture of what is in your mind.

Write a description. Be sure to give your reader enough details to form a clear picture. Remember to use adjectives (words that describe nouns). When you finish, make a list on a separate paper of the adjectives in your paragraph. Give your paragraph to a friend. Ask the friend to list the adjectives. Compare your list with your friend's list.

**Topics you might use:**
- your bike or your new shoes
- your favorite shirt or other piece of clothing
- your favorite sandwich or pizza
- your favorite place to play
- your pet, sister, brother, mom, or dad
- a room in your house
- the family car

**Topic sentence examples with suggested details:**

**Topic sentence:** Our family car is an old, green station wagon.
**Details:** *Does it have scratches or dents? Does it run well or make unusual sounds? How does the inside look?*

**Topic sentence:** My pet is a hamster named Snoopy.
**Details:** *Describe its looks (color, size, body). Why did you name your pet Snoopy? What are his habits?*

Now, prepare your own description. Write a topic sentence about your subject. Prepare a list of the details you will include.

**Topic sentence:** _____

_____

**Details:** _____

_____

Finally, write your paragraph from your notes above. Your detail ideas should become complete sentences.

_____

_____

Name _____  Date _____

# Story Beginnings

Read these story beginnings. List the characters, setting, and problem for each story.

The beginning of a story tells the **who** of the story. It should tell **where** and **when** the story takes place, and what is the problem.

The **characters** are the people or creatures the story is about.

The **setting** is where and when it takes place.

Robert and Kevin decided to camp out in Robert's backyard Saturday night. They set up the tent under a huge, old oak tree. The boys got into their warm bedrolls to go to sleep. Suddenly, something began hitting the roof of the tent.

**Characters:** _____
**Setting:** _____
**Problem:** _____

Sarah went to the park on a windy March day to fly her new kite. Just as she succeeded in getting the kite into the air, a big boy ran by. He grabbed the kite string and raced away with Sarah's kite.

**Characters:** _____

**Setting:** _____
**Problem:** _____

Now, write your own story beginning. List the characters, setting, and problem on another sheet of paper. Develop a paragraph to include all the information you have listed.

# Editing

There are many mistake in the sentences below. Cross out each letter that should be a capital. Write the capital above it. Put the correct punctuation mark at the end.

1. in june, we are out of school

2. which answer is right, bill

3. watch out for that snake

4. how do we get to the zoo

5. yesterday, janet baked brownies

6. the circus was so exciting

7. where are tom and sue

8. don't you tease my dog, sam

9. we went to the movie on saturday

10. was the spelling test hard

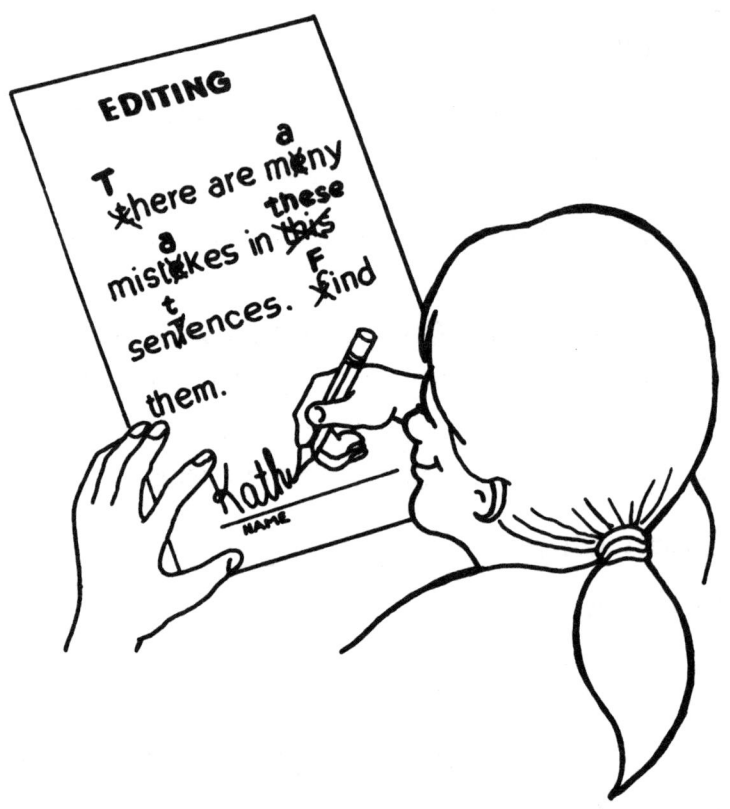

There are mistakes in the following paragraph. Rewrite it on another piece of paper. Edit for capitalization and punctuation. Remember to indent the first sentence. Leave out any sentence that does not tell about the topic sentence. Then, write another paragraph about games to play at a party. Edit your work.

Planning a birthday party can be fun first decide whom to invite Then send out invitation. choose the games to be played at the party My birthday is in August. get the refreshments ready. have fun when the guests arrive

Name _____   Date _____

# Introducing Me!

A good way for a group to get to know you is to tell about yourself. Use this form to help you get started.

My name is _____.

I am _____ years old. The most important thing about me is
_____.

I like to _____

and I am getting better at it all the time because I _____
_____.

Another thing that makes me happy is _____.

I do this _____.

A thing that is difficult for me is _____.

I try to be a good friend by _____.

It is important to me that people think of me as _____

and _____.

Add any additional information that may help other people understand you. Use the information from the form above to write a draft of a paragraph. Share your autobiography with the class.

On another sheet of paper, draw a self-portrait to go with your autobiography.

MP5095 - Reading and Writing                    Writing

# My Happiest Time

Remember a time when something wonderful happened?

Maybe that happy time was when you got something special for your birthday. You had wished for it but didn't think you would really get it. Or maybe it was when you found your lost puppy, after you thought you would never see him or her again!

1. Think of your happiest time. What was your experience?
   _____

2. Where were you when this happened? Describe the place in detail.
   _____

3. How did you feel inside when this happened?
   _____

4. What did you say when it happened?
   _____

5. Was anyone else there? _____

6. Did he or she help this happy time to happen? _____

7. What did you do after it happened? _____
   _____

8. Do you think this will be something you will remember when you grow up?
   _____

Write a thank you note to someone that was involved in your happiest time. Did you get a great birthday present from your aunt? Write a note telling her how much you loved the gift. Did you get an 'A' on a test? Write a letter to your teacher thanking him or her for teaching you the information.

# I Had a Dream

Everyone has dreams when they sleep. Sometimes dreams are scary, and sometimes they are so funny we wake up laughing. A dream may seem very real or make hardly any sense at all.

1. Think about a dream you can remember. Write a main idea sentence about the dream.
   _____
   _____

2. Tell what happened in your dream in the order in which things occurred. You may need to use signal words like first, next, then, and after that. Include details to make it interesting.
   _____
   _____
   _____
   _____
   _____
   _____

3. How did your dream end?
   _____
   _____
   _____
   _____

4. How do you feel about your dream now?
   _____
   _____
   _____
   _____

**EXTRA!** On another sheet of paper, write the beginning, middle, and end of your dream. Your feeling about the dream can go at the beginning or the end of your story.

# Your Lucky Day

Some people think things like four-leaf clovers, horseshoes, and rabbits' feet are good luck charms. Walking under a ladder, breaking a mirror, and seeing a black cat are thought to be unlucky.

Think about something that could happen to you or something that you could find that would be lucky. For example, good luck is hearing that your favorite team will be playing nearby on Friday night. Bad luck would be finding out that all the tickets to the game are sold.

Cut out the horseshoe shown here. Write your idea of good luck on one side. On the opposite side, write what could happen to turn your good luck into bad.

Name_____ Date _____

# Loyal Friends

Everyone needs to have friends. Have you thought about what having friends means?

It means having someone to share your free time with and having someone to talk to about your feelings. It means knowing that a person will care about you today, tomorrow, and next week too. Knowing you can trust a person to be nice to you day after day is called having a loyal friend!

1. List ways people you know show they are loyal friends.

   A. _____  B. _____
   C. _____  D. _____

2. List ways you are a loyal friend.

   A. _____  B. _____
   C. _____  D. _____

3. On another paper, write a draft of a paragraph about the ways you try to be a loyal friend. Choose a main idea sentence to start your paragraph. It might be something like this:

   Since I like to have loyal friends, I try to be a loyal friend.
   I try my best to be a loyal friend.

4. Use the ideas from your list to add three or four sentences telling ways you are a loyal friend. Have a friend read your paragraph to see if he or she has ideas about improving it. Write the final copy.

Write a brief biography of your best friend. Why do you like being friends with this person?

Name _____  Date _____

# Why Doesn't Someone Invent A Way To...

You may have said these words yourself. Someone was probably sweeping a rug or floor when he got the idea of a vacuum cleaner. Another person may have been washing dishes when the idea for a dishwasher came to her.

Think of some chores you do at home which take too much time, or that you do not like to do. How about a machine to help you at school or play?

1. Make a list of chores you have that you do not like to do. Make a check by the one you dislike the most.

   A. _____
   B. _____
   C. _____
   D. _____

2. Share your list. Find others who dislike the same chore. Form a group and talk about ideas you have to make this job easier or more fun.

3. Write a draft of a paragraph describing the job you don't like and the best idea your group had for a machine or tool to make the job easier or more fun. (Try to think of something other than a robot.) Include as many details as you can about your good idea.

   _____
   _____
   _____
   _____
   _____
   _____

# Changes Around Us

Have you heard the saying, "Nothing ever stays the same"? Sometimes we wish things would stay the same.

1. List things you can think of that stay the same.

   Examples: The sun rises and sets every day.
   We sleep every night.

   A. _____
   B. _____
   C. _____
   D. _____

2. Sometimes we want things to change. We are very happy when they do. List things you are happy about when they do change.

   Examples: You get a new puppy and he or she grows.
   You learn a new skill.

   A. _____
   B. _____
   C. _____
   D. _____

3. Make a star beside the thing you like best that stays the same. Do the same for the thing you like best that changes. Choose one of them as a topic for writing a draft of a paragraph below. Write a main idea sentence for your topic. Then write two reasons why you like the thing that changes or stays the same. Write a supporting detail sentence for each reason. You will have written a five-sentence paragraph.

_____
_____
_____
_____
_____

Name _____  Date _____

# You'll Never Believe What Happened...

Tall tales are stories that stretch the truth. Pecos Bill was a legendary cowboy who lived in the western United States. Other cowboys sat around the campfire at night, inventing stories about things Pecos Bill did. The tales grew and became more outrageous. Even today, there are tall tale contests in Texas in which people make up hard-to-believe stories.

1. Read a tale about Pecos Bill, Paul Bunyan, or another North American tall tale hero. Notice how the story begins with an ordinary problem and how the hero performs an exaggerated feat to solve the problem.

2. List events, contests, or problems in your school, town, or state. Put a check by the one you think is the most interesting.

   A. _____    B. _____
   C. _____    D. _____

3. List real people who could solve the problem. How about your teacher, a parent, or a well-known person in your town? You might even add yourself to the list. Choose one of these people to become your imaginary hero or heroine who can solve the problem through strength, intelligence, and/or skill.

Put a check by that name.

   A. _____    B. _____
   C. _____    D. _____
   E. _____    F. _____

 On another sheet of paper, write a tall tale. Start with the problem or situation you chose. Use the person you chose as the hero or heroine to find an unbelievable solution.

Name _____     Date _____

# Hobby Heaven

Hobby Heaven would be a place where you could have any hobby you want. Think about what you would like for a hobby if training, money, or time were not problems.

What kind of hobbies do your friends have? Have you read about interesting hobbies? Do you know some adults who have different and unusual hobbies? Ask your librarian for books about hobbies or check the internet for ideas.

1. What would you like as a hobby?
   _____

2. Why do you think this would be an interesting hobby?
   _____

3. Would this be a hobby which might become a paying job someday? Explain how.
   _____

4. Who might help you get started on this hobby? Name people who might help you get started.
   _____

5. Are there books to read on this hobby? Name them.
   _____

6. Is there a place where you can help another person with this hobby now?
   _____

7. Write the address of an internet site about this hobby.
   _____

Write a paragraph about what would be Hobby Heaven to you.

# Vegetable Soup

What if you were a vegetable, swimming in warm broth, just ladled into a soup bowl? This is your last chance to tell the story of your life.

1. List vegetables found in vegetable soup.

    A. _____  B. _____

    C. _____  D. _____

    E. _____  F. _____

2. Circle the one you would like to be. Give yourself a name like Tommy Tomato or Sally Celery.

    Write your new name. _____

3. To help you create a story, answer these questions.

    A. What stages did you go through as you were growing up?
    _____

    B. How did you get from the farm or garden to the store?
    _____

    C. Were you canned, frozen, or fresh?
    _____

    D. Who prepared you to go in the soup?
    _____

    E. Why are the vitamins and minerals you contain important to people?
    _____

Write a poem about your life as a vegetable. You may use any form of poetry, and you may want to look in books or other resources for help. Use your answers from this page to write your poem.

# Far-Out Notes

Congratulations! You have been selected to go into space for three days as the first student on a shuttle flight. The government has asked you to keep a journal of everything you see, hear, feel, smell, and do. On the lines below, write three journal entries. Imagine everything you do: your jobs, what you wear, what you eat, where you sleep, and the feeling of weightlessness. Describe the blast-off and landing. Imagine the good and the unpleasant parts of the voyage. Have a great trip into space!

First Day: _____

_____

_____

_____

_____

Middle Day: _____

_____

_____

_____

_____

Last Day: _____

_____

_____

_____

_____

Name_____    Date _____

# A School Pet

Do you have a pet at home or at school? Some classrooms do, but many do not. If you already have an animal or animals at home or school, think of a different animal you would like to have. If you don't have one now, try to think of a good pet.

1. Interview your teacher or parent to find out his or her feelings about pets. Write the question you want to ask.

   _____

2. Knowing how your teacher feels, think of an animal he or she might enjoy.

   _____

3. How much space would this animal need? Is a cage or aquarium available for this animal? If so, how much would it cost?

   _____

4. Is other equipment needed, such as an exercise ball or wheel? How much would it cost?

   _____

5. What does this animal eat? About how much would it cost to feed him or her for one month?

   _____

6. What is necessary to keep this animal clean and comfortable? Is there an expense for bedding for a month? Would you be able to do the work to keep this animal's cage clean?

   _____

   _____

Write a story for your teacher explaining what animal you would like to have as a class pet. Be sure to include why you want this animal, things you would need to buy to prepare for it, who would do the work, and how you would keep the animal clean and healthy.

Name_____  Date _____

# Days Gone By

How do you think your grandparents or great-grandparents lived as children? Do your grandparents talk to you about the way they lived? What things were the same then, and what things have changed a lot?

Make a list of the things you think have changed and a list of the things you think have stayed the same.

1. Things That Have Changed

   _____
   _____
   _____
   _____
   _____

2. Things That Have Stayed the Same

   _____
   _____
   _____
   _____
   _____

Research information about a historical figure that lived in the early 1900s. Write an article for a magazine or newspaper on the life of the person you selected.

MP5095 - Reading and Writing          103          Writing

Name_____   Date_____

# A Brave Moment

Sometimes you have to do things you dread or that you are afraid to do. You tell yourself to be brave and do your best, but it is scary! Maybe you have to tell your mom you broke something she loved. Perhaps you have to sing a solo in front of the music class.

1. Think of a situation you dreaded. What was it?

   _____

2. How did you feel? Were your hands or knees shaking?

   _____

3. What were you afraid might happen?

   _____

4. Was there anyone to encourage you? Who? What did this person do?

   _____

5. Were you able to do that thing you dreaded to do?

   _____

6. How did you feel when it was all over?

   _____

7. Would you do it differently next time?

   _____

8. What would you say or do to encourage a person in the same situation?

   _____

 Write a short paragraph explaining things you can do to stay calm in a situation like the one above.

# Lost, But Hopefully Found!

Everyone loses things from time to time. Have you lost something you cared about? Perhaps it was the money your grandma sent you for your birthday. Maybe you put your new coat down while playing and forgot to pick it up again.

1. Think of something you lost. Describe it in detail.

2. How did you feel when you realized it was gone?

3. Did the thing you lost belong to you or to someone else?

4. What did you do to try to find it?

5. Did anyone help you look for it?

6. Did you find it? Where was it?

7. How did you feel when you found it?

8. If you haven't found it yet, how are you feeling now?

Use the information on this page to write the story. The main idea sentence for the paragraph tells what you lost. The details for the paragraph are in sentences 2-8 above.

# Hats Tell Stories

Hats come in many shapes and sizes and colors.

1. Think about all the hats you've ever seen. Choose one hat and draw it in this box.

2. Think about who might wear this hat. How would he or she look, move, talk, and treat other people? Is this person male or female? Old or young? What would this person like to do or not do? What kind of job would this individual have? Would this person like a special sport? Imagine this person in your mind. It might help you to draw a picture of this person wearing this hat.

3. Write a descriptive paragraph about the person who wears this hat. Include answers to the questions above. Be sure to include any other details that would help describe this individual. Don't tell which hat you have chosen for the character you described.

4. When everyone has finished their descriptions, take turns reading the paragraphs. Guess what type of hat the described person would have worn.

Name _____  Date _____

# Your Writer's Daybook

Writers keep special journals and notebooks with them at all times to jot down ideas and notes that might come in handy when they are writing.

Many writers call this special book a "daybook" because they make it a habit to write in it everyday so they will have lots of ideas when they sit down to write.

It is a good idea to write down everything you see in detail because you never know when something will spark a writing idea. A sign tacked up on a telephone pole near your home telling of a lost pet might prompt you to write a story about a child who has to go away on a vacation while a pet ferret is missing. Or, seeing a bumper sticker advertising Jackson Hole, Wyoming might remind you of an exciting vacation you would like to write about.

To start keeping your daybook, find a notebook—any size will do. You can make your own by stapling together sheets of lined paper with construction paper for a cover, or by putting theme paper in a three-ring binder.

Write an entry for your daybook for a cold, January day with two feet of fresh snow on the ground.

_____
_____
_____

Write notes about the day you went to the zoo with your family.

_____
_____
_____
_____

Write what you might see during a walk around your house if you look very closely.

_____
_____
_____
_____

Name_____  Date_____

# Inventing Characters

Some writers say that characters are even more important to a story than a plot. They believe that if readers care about the characters, they will be eager to find out what happens to them. The better you know your characters, the easier it is to know what they will do next. Here is a form to help you invent characters and get to know about them.

If you can't think of an interesting name, this way always works. It is also fun! Get the white pages of your local telephone book. Go down the list of last names and find one you think is interesting. If you know a little about your character, you can try to match the last name with what you know. For instance, if your character is an Irish immigrant you will not want to use a name like McCafferty, which is Scottish, or Monet, which is French.

When you have chosen a last name, open the phone book to a different page and choose a first name that sounds good with it. Do not use the name of a real person. If the name you create turns out to be someone's name, it should have been an accident. Most fiction writers include a disclaimer at the beginning of each book that reads, "Any resemblance to persons living or dead is purely coincidental." People do not always enjoy seeing their names in print, especially if the characters bearing their names are not good and honest people.

Writer's Name:_____

## Character Invention Form

Character's name:_____ Nickname (if any) _____

Age: _____ Date of birth: _____

Address: _____

E-mail address _____

Description: _____

Eye color:_____ Hair color: _____

Height: _____ Weight: _____

Occupation:_____ and/or school grade: _____

Favorite color _____ Favorite hobby: _____

Interests: _____

Fears: _____

Favorite foods: _____

Best friend(s): _____

Name(s) of parent(s):_____

Siblings (brothers and/or sisters):_____

Other information: _____

# Hat Tricks

There are times in all writers' lives when original thoughts just don't come easily. If you're having trouble coming up with a new and different character it sometimes helps to throw yourself into the part! Here's how it works.

If you are at school, ask your teacher if he or she has a hat collection. Gather up some hats from the hall closet, the attic, the basement, or your bedroom. (Be sure to ask permission if the hats belong to someone else.) Or imagine yourself in one of the hats pictured at the bottom of the page. Answer the questions.

One person's collection of hats might include an army helmet, a baby's knit cap, a sailor cap, a golf cap, a sunbonnet, and a felt hat with a brim. Put one of the hats on your head and look in the mirror. Ask yourself some questions.

What kind of person am I? _____

What is my name? _____

What do I do for a living? _____

Where am I going in this hat? _____

Where do I live? _____

What do I like? _____

Put on a different hat and try to create a different character from the first. Then invent a situation in which the two characters would come together. Give each character a name. Write a dialogue between the two characters.

_____
_____
_____
_____
_____

Name_____    Date_____

# What's in a Name?

The names writers give to their characters are quite important to the stories. Can you imagine Pippi Longstocking as Pippi Baker? Or how about changing Tom Sawyer's name to Howard? Names are important because they give the reader extra clues about the characters.

You can practice naming a character. The first name we need is for a cowboy. Would you choose John Fairbanks, Kevin Johnson, or Bill Slade? The cowboy's real name might be Kevin Johnson, but it doesn't sound as much like a western name, so it's probably better to use Bill Slade.

The second character is a woman who is very rich and very spoiled. Would you name her Goldie Lockett, Beatrice Dunbury, or Lucy Foley? Goldie and Lucy sound like down-to-earth people, but Beatrice sounds as if she could be quite spoiled.

Make up names for the following characters.

a sheriff_____      a bank robber _____

a baseball player_____      a movie star _____

a Navy pilot_____       a teacher _____

a racehorse_____        a superhero _____

a doctor_____         a magician _____

Now, insert the names in the blanks of a play about a suspected bank robbery and see if you still like them.

**Sheriff** _____: (in a stern voice) Put up your hands!

**Masked man:** There must be some mistake. I am a movie star. My name is

_____, and I'm starring in this movie. It's about a bank robbery.

**Sheriff:** (scratching his chin) Hmmm. Is this the movie about the famous bank robber?

**Masked man:** (excited) Yes! That's the one! And, next month I play the magician in a new movie.

Did you like the way your names sounded? If not, try again.

Name _____   Date _____

# Look Who's Talking

To write realistic dialogue, you should listen closely to the many conversations going on around you every day. Begin jotting down, as closely as possible, the exact words and phrases you hear.

Listen to the various ways people talk to different people. A teacher may sound one way when he or she addresses a class, and another when talking to the principal. Listen to your fellow students on the playground and in the cafeteria. Try to overhear conversations in stores and movie theaters. The more you listen the better your details will be when you write your own dialogue.

Keep a Dialogue Diary. Write down snatches of conversation as close as possible to the exact wording. Remember to place quotation marks around the words that are spoken.

Example: "Tom, where is your homework?" asked Mr. Gold.

Dialogue One: _____

_____

_____

_____

_____

_____

_____

Dialogue Two: _____

_____

_____

_____

_____

_____

_____

After you have collected several sets of actual dialogue, try your luck at writing some. Think of two characters and write a dialogue between them.

Character 1: _____
Character 2: _____
Character 1: _____
Character 2: _____

Now read your dialogue aloud and see if it sounds authentic (true to the characters). Do the words and phrases sound correct for the age of the characters? How could you make the dialogue more believable?

# The Music I Like Best

Because there are so many kinds of music and so many musicians, we have a wide variety from which to choose. Your favorites are probably not the same as your parents'. Your favorites may or may not be the same as your friends'.

1. What kind of music do you like best? _____
   _____

2. Who is your favorite group or individual musician? _____
   _____

3. Why do you particularly like this musician or group? _____
   _____

4. How do you listen to this music? (radio, CD player, etc.) _____
   _____

5. What CDs by this group or person do you own? _____
   _____

6. Which song or recording do you like best? _____
   _____

7. Use the information above to write a draft of a paragraph about your favorite music.

8. Share a tape or CD by your favorite musicians with friends or classmates. Read your paragraph. Then play your favorite song.

Name_____   Date _____

# Memory Writing

Powerful writing can come from memories. Anything which has already happened is a memory. Your memories might be five years old or one minute old. Your mind is full of memories that can provide thousands of writing ideas.

Some people say they can remember all the way back to their first year of life. How far back do your memories go? You may find that the more you exercise your memory, the more you will remember.

How many memories can you bring back? Fill in the blanks and let the memories roll!

The first thing I remember was _____
_____

The first house I remember any details about was _____
_____

A pet I remember was _____
One friend I had was _____
My first memory of school was _____
_____

When I was little I used to _____
_____

One toy I remember playing with was _____
On holidays, I used to _____
_____

Now, choose one of your memories and write as much as you can about it. Don't worry about spelling and punctuation until you have written down all you can remember.

_____
_____
_____
_____

Can you think of a way this memory could be used in a story? Here's an example: One writer remembered being stung by a hornet as he stepped into his shoes while dressing for a birthday party. He decided to use the hornet in a story he was writing, but he placed it in a lunchbox instead of a shoe. You can change any of your memories to suit your story. On another sheet of paper, write a fiction story based on your memory.

Name_____  Date _____

# What If?

Sometimes, it seems fictional stories simply pour out of our brains onto paper. At other times, we draw a blank. That is when the 'what ifs' come in handy. You can use the 'what ifs' in many ways to create plots and move the action along in your stories.

Pretend that you have created a character named Sandy. Sandy is a seven-year-old girl because you have a sister who is seven and you know a lot about kids who are seven. Suddenly, you find yourself stuck. What about Sandy? All you can think of is your own sister and nothing seems exciting. This is the time to use the 'what ifs.' What if Sandy got lost? What if she got stuck inside something? What if she got lost while on vacation with her family?

Or, what if Sandy had something about her that made her different from any other sister in the world. What if Sandy were really an alien? What if her parents didn't know it? What if her brother found out?

Now it's your turn. Use Sandy or your own character. Start by writing a little about your character.

Character's Name:_____
Age: _____
Description: _____
_____

What if _____
What if _____
What if _____
What if _____

After you have filled in all the blanks above, choose one or more of the 'what ifs' and begin to write about it. Don't worry about spelling or punctuation until you have completed the writing. You can edit your writing later.

_____
_____
_____
_____
_____

Now, read over what you wrote and write a new set of 'what ifs.'
What if _____
What if _____
What if _____
What if _____

Name _____  Date _____

# Combining Ideas

There are several ways to combine sentence ideas.

- You can combine adjectives.
  **Example:** The friendly man waved to us. The young man waved to us.
  The friendly, young man waved to us.

- You can combine adverbs.
  **Example:** The painters worked slowly. The painters worked carefully.
  The painters worked slowly and carefully.

- You can combine groups of words that tell where, when, and how (prepositional phrases).
  **Example:** The tree fell over last night. The tree fell into our yard.
  The tree fell over last night into our yard.

- You can combine subjects.
  **Example:** Squirrels scampered across the lawn. Rabbits scampered across the lawn.
  Squirrels and rabbits scampered across the lawn.

- You can combine predicates.
  **Example:** The waiter took our order. The waiter brought our food.
  The waiter took our order and brought our food.

*Now, combine each pair of sentences into a single sentence.*

1. Mother washed my clothes. Mother dried my clothes.
   _____

2. The children raked leaves. The children washed windows.
   _____

3. Sue played in the band. Rich played in the band.
   _____

4. The boy broke his arm yesterday. He broke his arm at the skating rink.
   _____

5. It was a clear day. It was a breezy day.
   _____

6. The movie was too long. It was boring.
   _____

7. The farmer will give the animals food. He will give them water.
   _____

8. Elaine spoke loudly. She spoke clearly.
   _____

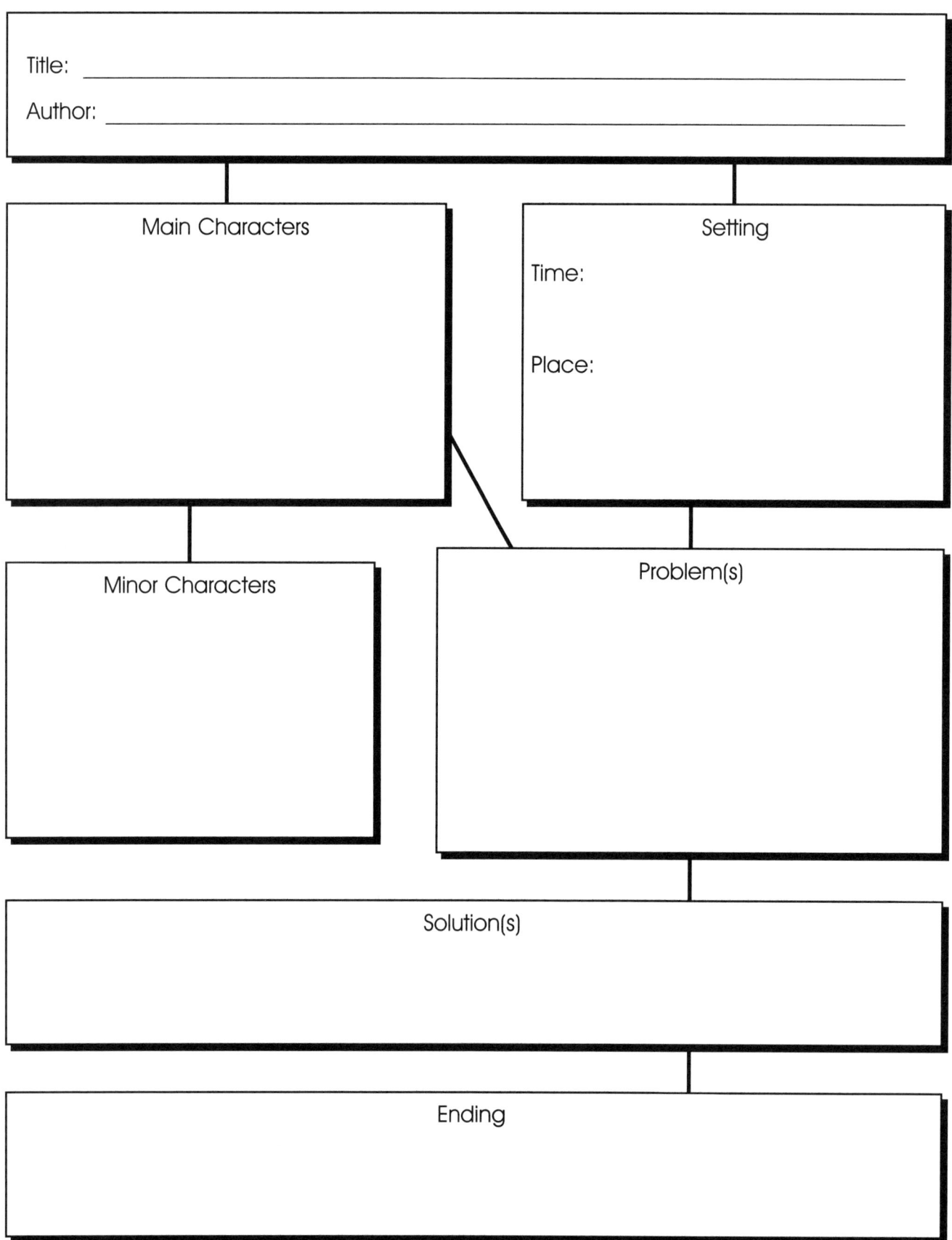

Name _____    Date _____

# Story Frame

Title: _____

Author: _____

This story is mainly about _____
                              (name of main character)

Other important characters are _____
_____

This story takes place (when and where) _____
_____
_____
_____
_____

The problem is _____
_____
_____
_____

The problem is solved when _____
_____
_____
_____

At the end of the story _____
_____
_____
_____
_____

Name_____  Date _____

# The ABCs of Rhyming

Writing poems that rhyme can be easy and fun. There are two ways to make rhyming easy. The first is to use a rhyming dictionary. This type of dictionary is alphabetized according to the sound of the words. If you were looking for a word that rhymed with "page," you would look under "age," and you would find words like "cage," "gauge," and "rage."

The second way is to write out ABCs on the top of a sheet of paper. Then take the sound of the word you want to rhyme and put it behind each consonant in the alphabet until you find the word you like best.

Example: "The baby rhino sat on a cat" is the first line. Before writing the second line you need to know what possible rhyming words you can use. Go to the alphabet and start putting "at" with the consonants.

B C D E F G H J K L M N P Q R S T V W X Y Z

You see that you can make bat, brat, chat, fat, flat . . . Yes! Let's try "flat."

The baby rhino sat on a cat.
Now the cat's extremely flat!
I hope he never sits on me.
I don't want to be as flat as a key!

It's your turn to do some quick rhymes. Here are the first and third lines for your first poem.

I saw a gorilla asleep in a cave.
_____

I ran away as fast as I could
_____

Now, write all four lines.
_____
_____
_____
_____

Dr. Seuss has delighted us with his nonsense rhymes. Try your luck at a four-line nonsense poem. You may use the first line below or write your own.

There's a zoozle living in my house!
_____
_____
_____
_____

Name_____ Date _____

# Thunderstorm of Poems

A thunderstorm always gets people's attention. Some people are terrified when wind, rain, thunder, and lightning happen at once. Others think it is very exciting and love to watch. Writing poetry is a very good way to express your feelings about a thunderstorm.

1. Brainstorm for nouns that come to mind when you think of thunderstorms. Circle the one you like best.

_____  _____  _____  _____

2. Write the word vertically on the lines below. Underline and capitalize each letter. Next to each letter, write a word starting with that letter that describes the noun. If you have trouble thinking of adjectives that begin with that letter, look in a dictionary.

Example:

**W** ild
**I** cy
**N** aughty
**D** eafening
**WIND!**

3. Rewrite your poem using phrases instead of single words.

Example:

**W** ild and ferocious
**I** cy daggers sting
**N** aughty gusts chase the leaves
**D** eafening howls ring
**WIND!**

Write a poem using your name. Use the same poetry style shown above.

Name _____  Date _____

# Peel Me a Poem

Poetry can be fun to write if you enjoy playing with words. The sound of the words is as important as the rhythm of the line. Some words will sound more interesting than others. Some writers like to use lists in their poems. The poem below uses the names of states or cities and the days of the week.

Sunday in Saratoga,
Monday in Maine,
Tuesday in Tallahassee,
Wednesday in Spain,
Thursday in Nebraska,
Friday in L.A.,
Saturday in Canada,
That's all I have to say.

A poet might list nouns having to do with cooking and verbs having to do with baseball.

**Food Nouns**
pasta    pastry
salt     vegetables
pepper   crust
pan      spice
stove    dessert

**Baseball Verbs**
coach    hit
run      swing
catch    walk
throw    strike
lose     bat

A poem made by combining these is shown below

Pasta and peppers thrown
From a roadside stand
Hit the pan and
Strike the old iron stove.

Vegetables swing
From a crust of spice
As salty meat
Wins us dessert!

Poetry doesn't always have to have a deep meaning. It can be fun to play with words and see what happens. Make some lists and play with poetry. Choose two categories of your own or write more sports words and food words. You could write food verbs and baseball nouns!

**Nouns**                              **Verbs**
_____  _____         _____  _____
_____  _____         _____  _____
_____  _____         _____  _____
_____  _____         _____  _____
_____  _____         _____  _____

Write a poem using words from the two lists. Be playful with the words and don't worry about making too much sense. Listen to the sounds of the words as you try them out in various ways.

_____
_____

# Cinquain Poems

Puppies

Cuddly, innocent

Tumbling, chewing, licking

Ready to give love

Pups

This poem is called a cinquain. It is written in a special way.

**Line 1**—one noun for the subject

**Line 2**—two words describing the subject

**Line 3**—three words showing actions of the subject

**Line 4**—four words expressing feeling about the subject

**Line 5**—a synonym for the subject

1. Follow the guidelines. Write a cinquain on the lines. Capitalize the first word of each line. Use commas between words in a series. Animals make good subjects, but your poem may be about anything you wish.

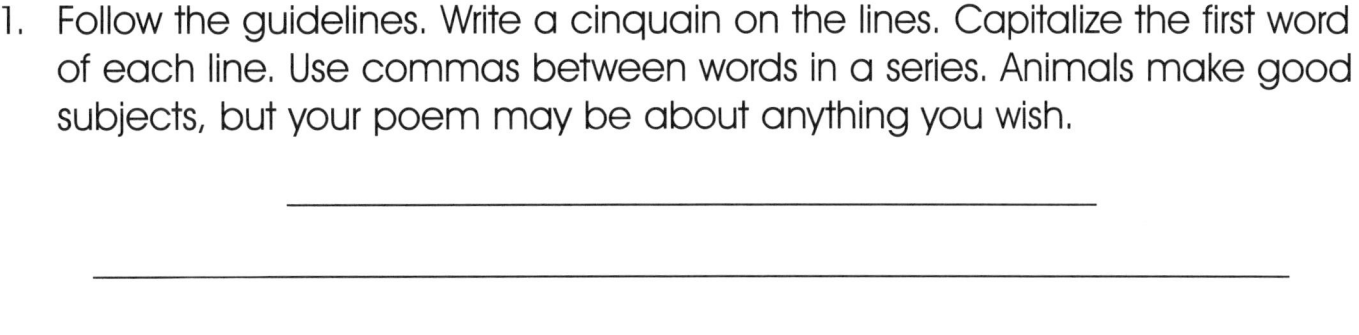

2. Read your poem aloud to a friend to see if it sounds right. Copy and illustrate it. Poems are meant to be spoken aloud, so perhaps you can memorize and say it to your class.

# V.I.P.

The initials V.I.P. usually stand for Very Important Person. You can become a V.I.P.—a **V**ery **I**mportant **P**oet—by following this guideline for writing initial poems.

Write the initials of your first, middle, and last names as shown below. Then, brainstorm for colorful words and phrases that begin with each initial. If you have difficulty thinking of interesting phrases, glance through several books by well-known authors or poets to see how they use colorful language.

| **S** | **R** | **M** |
|---|---|---|
| Sky skimmers | Rain's loud fury | Much-lived life |
| Scent of autumn | Racing ahead | Mournful eyes |
| Shadows of trees | Rustling of leaves | Memories like these |
| _____ | _____ | _____ |
| _____ | _____ | _____ |
| _____ | _____ | _____ |

Choose a phrase from the first column, one from the second, and one from the third that would be meaningful together. Write the chosen phrases to make a poem.

Example:
Scent of autumn
Rustling of leaves
Memories like these

_____
_____
_____

# New Rhymes From Old

Write the words of any short rhyming poem you know. It could be a nursery rhyme or other type. You can copy one from a book if you'd like.

_____
_____
_____
_____
_____

Rewrite the poem using the same rhythm and rhyme scheme, but change several of the words to make a new poem.

Example based on Hickory, Dickory, Dock:

> Gallop, a-gallop, a-gill,
> A horse ran over a hill.
> The horse said, "Neigh,
> I cannot stay."
> Gallop, a-gallop, a-gill.

Write your poem.

_____
_____
_____
_____
_____

Write a title for your poem.

_____

Use the poetry style above to write a poem about your favorite school subject.

# Nonsense Verse

Nonsense verses are silly, rhyming poems that sometimes use made-up words.

**The Eel**

I don't mind eels
Except as meals
And the way they feels.

*Ogden Nash*

Finish each line by writing words and phrases that rhyme. Made-up words are great.

If you ever go to Buffalo
Be sure to see _____.

My dear grandpa snores so loud
_____.

One day an alien visited me
_____.

One, two, three, four,
_____.

I like camels, giraffes, and llamas
_____.

Once I saw a rainbow stretch across the sky
_____.

# Answer Key

**Page 3**
A. 1. curious
   2. snoopy
   3. nosy
B. 1. nosy, curious, snoopy
   2. curious
   3. nosy
   4. curious (2) nosy (1), snoopy (3)

**Page 4**
A. 1. dreadful
   2. frightening
   3. horrible
B. 1. dreadful, frightening, horrible
   2. horror-horrible
      dread-dreadful
      fright-frightening

**Page 5**
A. 1. wise
   2. clever
   3. sly
B. 1. sly, wise, clever
   2. Answers may vary
   3. clever (3), sly (2), wise (1)

**Page 6**
A. 1. peered
   2. gazed
   3. glimpsed
B. 1. glimpse
   2. peer
   3. gaze
C. glimpse (2), gaze (1), peer (3)

**Page 7**
A. 1. complain
   2. worry
   3. fret
B. 1. complain
   2. fret
   3. worry

**Page 8**
A. 1. mischief
   2. trick
   3. pranks
B. 1. Mischief
   2. trick
   3. prank

**Page 9**
A. 1. surprise
   2. amaze
   3. astonishment
B. 1. astonish
   2. amaze
   3. surprise

**Page 10**
A. 1. curious
   2. clever
   3. gazed
   4. fret
   5. mischief
   6. astonishment
B. 1. snoopy
   2. wise
   3. worry
   4. prank
   5. sly
   6. nosy
   7. amaze
   8. trick
   9. clever
   10. fret
C. 1. amaze, clever, dreadful, fret
   2. mischief, nosy, peered, snoopy

**Page 11**
   3. curious, frightening, glimpsed, horrible
   4. prank, surprise, trick, wise
D. **Across**
   4. worry
   5. astonish
   8. gazed
   9. complain
   11. dreadful
   12. peered
   13. nosy
   14. curious
   15. clever
   16. mischief
   **Down**
   1. fret
   2. prank
   3. trick
   4. wise
   5. amazed
   6. sly
   7. snoopy
   8. glimpsed
   10. surprise

**Page 12**
A. 1. fleet
   2. admiral
   3. launch
B. 1. launch
   2. fleet
   3. launch
   4. admiral
C. 1. Launch
   2. fleet
   3. admiral

**Page 13**
A. 1. faithful
   2. loyal
   3. true
B. 1. loyal, true
   2. true
   3. faithful
   4. loyal

**Page 14**
A. 1. desired
   2. craved
   3. required
B. 1. craved
   2. desired, required
   3. require
   4. desire
C. 1. crave
   2. require
   3. require
   4. crave
   5. require
   6. require

**Page 15**
A. 1. squeak
   2. squeal
   3. squawk
B. 1. squawk, squeal, squeak
   2. squawk squeak, squeal
C. 1. squeal
   2. squawk
   3. squeak
D. 1. squeal
   2. squeak
   3. squawk
   4. squeal
   5. squeak

**Page 16**
A. 1. ill
   2. healthy
   3. ailing
B. 1. ailing
   2. ill
   3. healthy
   4. ail, health
C. 1. ailing
   2. ill
   3. healthy

**Page 17**
A. 1. squeak
   2. shed
   3. launch
   4. craved
   5. scale
   6. loyal
   7. ailing
   B. 1. loyal
   2. true
   3. craved
   4. required
   5. squawk
   6. squeal
   7. squeak
   8. healthy
   9. scale
   10. ailing
   11. ill
   12. shed

**Page 18**
A. 1. auditorium
   2. audio
   3. audience
B. 1. audience
   2. auditorium
   3. audio
C. 1. audience
   2. audio
   3. auditorium

**Page 19**
A. 1. starboard
   2. bow
   3. deck
B. 1. deck
   2. starboard
   3. bow
C. 1. b, a
   2. a, b

**Page 20**
A. 1. voyage
   2. safari
   3. expedition
B. 1. voyage
   2. safari
   3. expedition
C. 1. voyage
   2. expedition
   3. safari
**Across**
   2. expedition
   3. safari
**Down**
   1. voyage

**Page 21**
A. 1. moat
   2. Furrows
   3. trench
B. 1. furrow
   2. moat
   3. trench
C. trench, moat, furrows
   The men saw a fort.

**Page 22**
A. 1. misfortune
   2. calamity
   3. trouble
B. 1. misfortune
   2. trouble
   3. calamity
C. 1. calamity
   2. trouble
   3. misfortune
   4. calamity
   5. misfortune
   6. trouble
Note: text supports the choices given, but allow students to defend their answers.

**Page 23**
A. 1. execute
   2. achieve
   3. realized
B. 1. realized
   2. achieve
   3. execute
C. 1. b
   2. a

**Page 24**
A. 1. digest
   2. summary
   3. brief
Note: lawyers' children may know brief as a noun.
B. 1. brief
   2. summary
   3. digest
C. brief:
   1. b
   2. a
   digest:
   3. a
   4. b

**Page 25**
A. 1. audience
   2. deck (or bow)
   3. voyage
   4. expedition (or safari)
   5. misfortune
   6. achieve
   7. digest
B. 1. audio
   2. starboard
   3. expedition
   4. trench
   5. calamity
   6. realized
   7. summary

**Page 26**
A. 1. sustain
   2. maintain
   3. prolong
B. 1. prolong
   2. maintain
   3. sustain
C. 1. sustain
   2. maintain
   3. prolong

**Page 27**
A. 1. toddlers
   2. youth
   3. adult
B. 1. toddler
   2. adult
   3. youth
C. toddler—ride a tricycle
      sit in a high chair
   adult—be a teacher
      drive a taxi
   youth—go to high school
      be a scout member

**Page 28**
A. 1. boulder
   2. pebbles
   3. gravel
B. 1. pebbles
   2. gravel
   3. boulder
C. pebbles, boulder, gravel
   People value our world

**Page 29**
A. 1. fragrance
   2. scent
   3. aroma
B. 1. aroma
   2. fragrance
   3. scent
C. 1. aroma
   2. scent
   3. fragrance

**Page 30**
A. 1. lichen
   2. ferns
   3. moss
B. 1. moss
   2. ferns
   3 lichen
C. 1. lichen
   2. moss
   3. ferns

**Page 31**
A. 1. display
   2. exposed
   3. disclose
B. 1. disclose
   2. display
   3. exposed
C. aroma, disclose, display, exposed, ferns, lichen, moss, scent

**Page 32**
A. 1. justice
   2. liberated
   3. freedom
B. 1. justice
   2. liberated
   3. freedom
C. justice, liberated, freedom
   liberty for all

**Page 33**
A. 1. sustain
   2. toddlers
   3. boulder
   4. aroma
   5. moss
   6. exposed
   7. justice
B. 1. maintain
   2. youth
   3. pebbles
   4. fragrance
   5. adult
   6. disclose
   7. liberated

**Page 34**
A. 1. dreary
   2. gloomy
   3. cheerful
B. 1. dreary
   2. gloomy
   3. cheerful
C. 1. happy, merry, jolly, smile, grin
   2. sad, dismal, frown, dreary, pout

**Page 35**
A. 1. formula
   2. recipe
   3. prescription
B. 1. prescription
   2. formula
   3. recipe
C. 1. recipe
   2. formula
   3. prescription

**Page 36**
A. 1. accurate
   2. exacting
   3. error
B. 1. error
   2. exacting
   3. accurate
C. accurate, error, exacting
   I can crack our code

**Page 37**
A. 1. gas
   2. fluids
   3. solid
B. 1. solid
   2. gas
   3. fluids
C. 1. fluids
   2. gas
   3. solid

**Page 38**
A. 1. nutritious
   2. inhale
   3. wholesome
B. 1. inhale
   2. wholesome
   3. nutritious
C. inhale, nutritious, wholesome

**Page 39**
A. 1. responsible
   2. negligent
   3. certain
B. 1. responsible
   2. negligent
   3. certain
C. 1. certain
   2. responsible
   3. negligent

**Page 40**
A. 1. cheerful
   2. formula
   3. exacting
   4. solid
   5. inhale
   6. certain
B. 1. gloomy
   2. recipe
   3. accurate
   4. fluids
   5. nutritious
   6. responsible

# Page 41
C. 1. gloomy
2. accurate
3. solid
4. negligent

D. **Across**
4. nutritious
6. recipe
9. fluids
10. gas
12. prescription
14. exacting
15. dreary

**Down**
1. inhale
2. error
3. negligent
5. solid
6. responsible
7. cheerful
8. gloomy
11. accurate
13. certain

# Page 42
1. 2, 3, 1
2. Glucose, sucrose, lactose, fructose (honey and corn syrup also contain sugar)
3. Answers will vary.

# Page 43
1. C
2. Aquamarine, sapphire, turquoise
3. Both are shades of red.
4. 16th century
5. Answers will vary.

# Page 44
1. Sweden, Denmark, Norway, and Iceland
2. to walk through deep snow
   to hear wolves
   to protect them from harsh weather and insect bites
   to smell danger

# Page 45
1. A
2. Answers will vary.

# Page 46

| | Asian | African | Both |
|---|---|---|---|
| Has tusks | | | X |
| Has two fingerlike extensions on end of trunk | | X | |
| Has one fingerlike extensions on end of trunk | X | | |
| Has larger ears | | X | |
| Has smoother forehead | | X | |
| Has two humps on forehead | X | | |
| Has looser, more wrinkled skin | | X | |
| Is smaller | X | | |

# Page 47
**Washington Monument**
Washington, D.C.
555'
brick and concrete
1888

**Statue of Liberty**
New York Harbor
305' (statue + base + stand)
steel and copper
1886

# Page 48
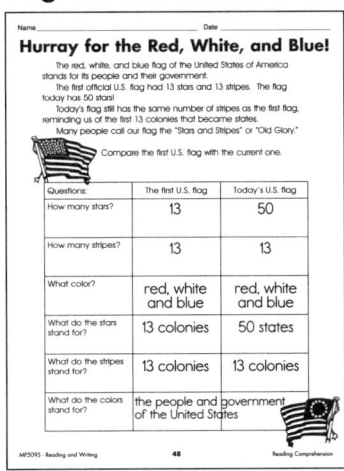

# Page 49

# Page 50
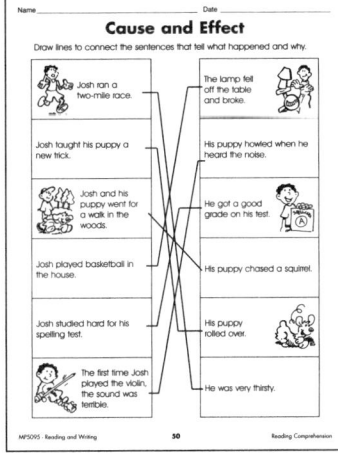

# Page 51
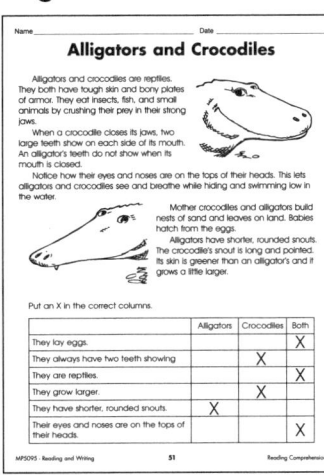

# Page 52
A. 2   B. 5   C. 10   D. 11
E. 7   F. 6   G. 16   H. 8
I. 3   J. 12  K. 15   L. 9
M. 4   N. 1   O. 13   P. 14

# Page 53
1. He fell off the covered wagon while crossing the Pecos River.
2. Chuck showed him his reflection in the water.

# Page 54
1. Alec, the elephant, lives there.
2. Mr. Grey, the custodian
3. Answers will vary.
4. No

# Page 55
1. to prevent someone or something from coming or going
2. moving, usually with an engine
3. weight

# Page 56
1. To share her vacation experience with family and friends
2. bears, elk, bison, big horn sheep
3. Because the mountains are so high

# Page 57
1. firelight, candles, torches, lanterns (also sunlight, starlight, moonlight)
2.-4. Answers will vary.

# Page 58
1. To protect him because he believed Merlin's prophesy.
2. b
3. a
4. covered with
5. created, prepared

# Page 59
1. Camels are well suited to desert life.
2. They have wide feet with thick pads.
3. to store food

# Page 60
1. strings, woodwinds, brass, and percussion
2. by blowing into a mouthpiece
3. trombone
4. tuba

# Page 61
1. strings
2. brass
3. brass
4. brass
5. strings

| Bow | Plucked |
|---|---|
| violin | guitar |
| viola | banjo |
| cello | mandolin |
| bass | ukulele |
| | harp |

# Page 62
1. wood
2. flute, piccolo, saxophone
3. Sound: By blowing air into a hole or over a vibrating reed
   Notes: By opening and closing holes
4. Answers will vary.

## Page 63

| Brass | Strings |
|---|---|
| trumpet | violin |
| cornet | viola |
| French horn | cello |
| baritone | bass |
| trombone | guitar |
| tuba | ukelele |

| Woodwinds | Percussion |
|---|---|
| flute | drums |
| piccolo | xylophone |
| clarinet | maracas |
| oboe | cymbals |
| bassoon | tambourine |
| saxophone | triangle |
| mandolin | bells |
| banjo | gong |
|  | harp |

## Page 64
1. Proposing a plan is easier than putting into action.
2. and 3. Answers will vary.

## Page 66
A. 
1. steak
2. hair
3. mail
4. waist
5. sun

B. 
1. steak, stake
2. hare, hair
3. mail, male
4. waste, waist
5. sun, son

## Page 67
A. 
1. sent
2. cent
3. scent
4. sent, cents, scent
5. due
6. do
7. dew
8. Do, dew, due
9. fowl
10. foul
11. fowl, foul

## Page 68
A. 1–4. shed
B. Answers will vary.
C. 
1. c
2. d
3. a
4. b

## Page 69
A. 1–4. scale
B. Answers will vary.
C. 
1. b
2. c
3. d
4. a

## Page 70
A. Answers will vary.
B. 
1. apple of my eye
2. an apple a day…
3. American as apple pie
4. There's a bad apple in every barrel.

## Page 87:
Rule 1: day, year; Rule 2: city, state; Rule 3: greeting, closing; Rule 4: on the right half of the paper (accept other wording of this idea)
Beginnings of paragraphs
Yes
No

## Page 89
Characters: Robert and Kevin; Setting: Robert's backyard on a Saturday night. Problem: Something is hitting the roof of the tent.
Characters: Sarah and a boy. Setting: March in the park.
Problem: A boy took Sarah's kite.

## Page 90
1. In June, we are out of school.
2. Which answer is right, Bill?
3. Watch out for that snake!
4. How do we get to the zoo?
5. Yesterday, Janet baked brownies.
6. The circus was so exciting!
7. Where are Tom and Sue?
8. Don't you tease my dog, Sam!
9. We went to the movie on Saturday.
10. Was the spelling test hard?

Planning a birthday party can be fun. First, decide whom to invite. Then send out invitations. Choose the games to be played at the party. Get the refreshments ready. Have fun when the guests arrive.

## Page 115
Answers may vary.
1. Mother washed and dried my clothes.
2. The children raked leaves and washed windows.
3. Sue and Rich played in the band.
4. The boy broke his arm yesterday at the skating rink.
5. It was a clear, breezy day.
6. The movie was too long and boring.
7. The farmer will give the animals food and water.
8. Elaine spoke loudly and clearly.